Reasonably Raw™

Inspiring YOU to Eat *more* Raw Food with Raw Chef Wendy

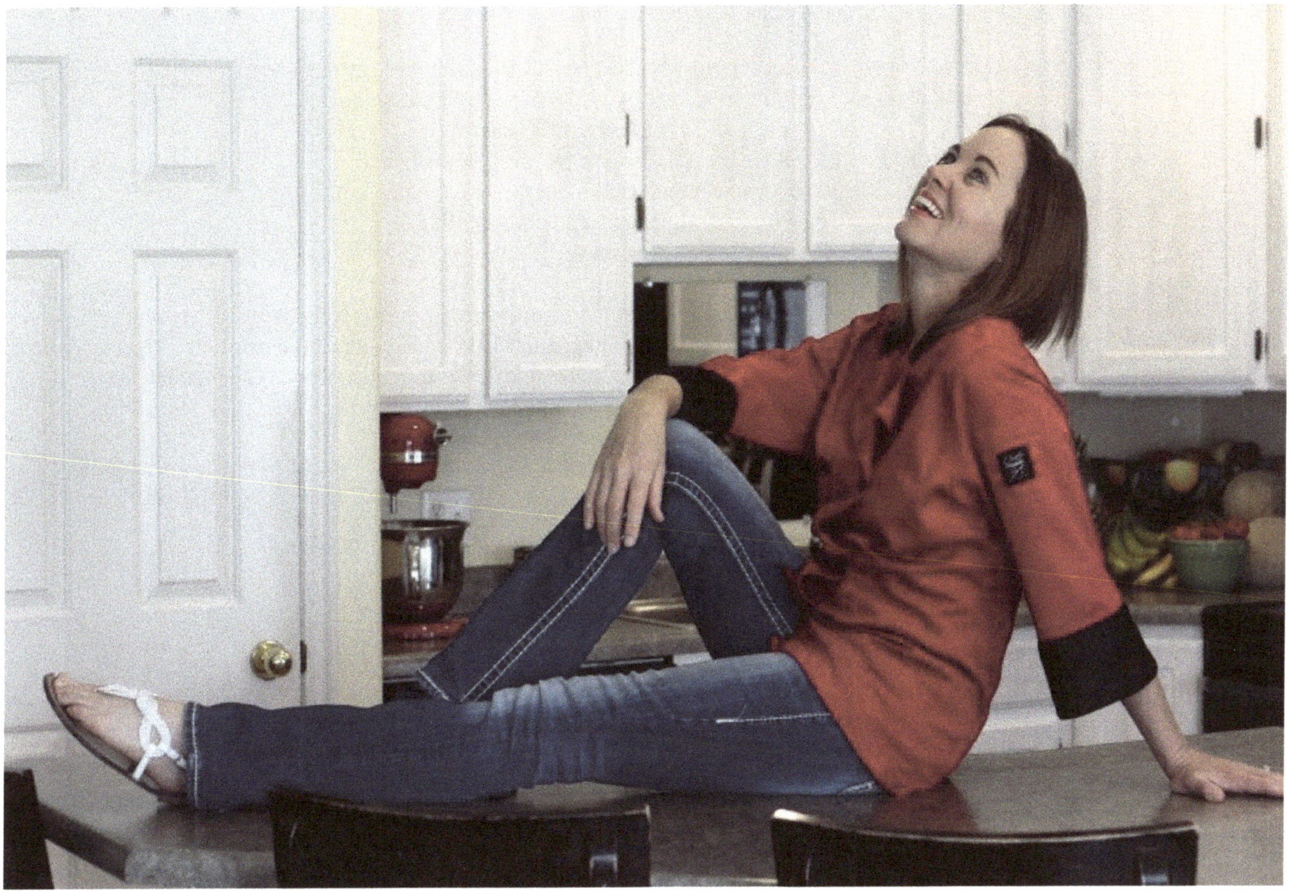

HAWAII WAY PUBLISHING

HAWAII WAY PUBLISHING
4118 West Harold Ct., Visalia, CA 93291
www.HAWAIIWAYPUBLISHING.com

HAWAII Way logo and name/acronym (Health and Wealth and Inspired Ideas)
are registered and trademarked by HAWAII Way Publishing.
Copyright © *2016 Wendy P. Thueson*
The right of *Wendy P.Thueson* to be identified as the
author of the work has been asserted by her in accordance with
the Copyright, Designs and Patents Act 1988
All rights reserved.

No part of this publication may be reproduced, distributed or transmitted in any form or by any means, including photocopying, recording or other electronic or mechanical methods without the prior and express written permission of the author or publisher, except in the case of brief quotations embodied in critical reviews and certain other noncommercial uses permitted by copyright law.

HAWAII Way Author/Speakers Agency can send authors to your live event. For more information or to book an event contact HAWAII Way Publishing at: HAWAIIWaypublishing@gmail.com, or 559-972-4168

Printed in the United States of America

ISBN 978-1-945384-04-2

Copyright © Raw Chef Wendy, LLC 2013, Eagle Mountain, UT, USA

First edition published in Utah by Wendy P. Thueson, Raw Chef Wendy, LLC in 2016
Author may be contacted at rawchefwendy@gmail.com
Photography by Heather Walker Studios and Raw Chef Wendy, LLC

Disclaimer:

The techniques and advice described in this book are a representation of the author's opinions based on her personal experience and are not in any way intended to diagnose, treat, prescribe, or cure any condition you may be experiencing. The author does not in any way claim responsibility for any liability, loss or risk, personal or otherwise, which is incurred as a result of using any of the techniques, recipes or recommendations suggested herein. If in any doubt, or if medical advice is required, please contact the appropriate health practitioner or professional.

TABLE OF CONTENTS

Welcome from the Author	8-9
Reasonably Raw Information	10-11
Tips for Success	12
7 Steps to Conscious Eating	13-14
What Cravings May Mean	13
The Kitchen	15-21
Natural Fruit and Vegetable Wash	21
Ideas to Inspire	22-23
Reasonably Raw Recipes	24

BEVERAGES

Wendy's Green Smoothie	25
Wendy's Fall Green Smoothie	25
Orange Julius	26
Watermelon Slushy	26
Almond Milk	26

BREAKFAST

Muesli	27
Baked Apple and Cranberry Oatmeal	27
Almost Raw Granola Bars	28
Huevos Rancheros	29
Crust-less Quiche	29
Crust-less Spinach Quiche	30
Breakfast Egg and Vegetable Mixture/Breakfast Burritos	31
Orzo Fritatta	32
Rainbow Frittata	33

SUBSTITUTIONS

Egg Substitution	34
Sugar Substitutions	34
Date Paste	34
Wendy's Gluten-Free Cake Flour Mix	35
Basic Raw Bread	35

NATURAL YEAST BREADS

Feeding Natural Yeast	36
Natural Yeast Bread Dough	36
Natural Yeast Pizza	37
Multi-Grain Roasted Flax and Pumpkin Seed Loaf	38
Storing Natural Yeast	38

SOUPS

Kale & Butternut Squash Soup	39
Lentil Soup	39-40
Wendy's Version of Zuppa Toscana	40
Wendy's Vegetarian Version of Wendy's® Restaurant Chili	41
Zucchini Basil Soup	41
Refrigerator Soup	42
Massaman Curry	43
Massaman Curry Paste	44
Potato Soup	45
New England Clam Chowder	46
Toscano Soup	46
Chicken Noodle Soup	47
Gluten-Free Egg Noodles	47
Vegetable Soup	48
Chicken Tortilla Soup	49

SALADS & DRESSINGS

Cran-Orange Quinoa Salad	50
Green Cranberry Salad & Dressing	51
Mediterranean Salad	52
Mediterranean Tuna Salad	52
Artichoke Pasta Salad	53
Pomegranate Salad & Dressing	54
Sweet Potato Salad Bowl	55
Caprece Summer Salad	56
Roasted Garlic Lemon Vinaigrette	57
Warm Brussel Sprouts Salad	57
Three Bean Salad	58
Fruit Salad with Strawberry Ginger Dressing	58
Potato and Lentil Salad	59
Quinoa, Kale & Butternut Squash Salad	59

SNACKS & SIDES

Café-Rio® Style Black Beans	60
Roasted Garlic Potatoes	60
Mediterranean Couscous	61
Chicken Waldorf Snackers	61
Tomato & Zucchini Bake	62
Cilantro Lime Rice	63
Warm Artichoke Dip	63
Marge's Nachos	64
Nachos with White Sauce	65
Tortilla Pockets	66
Twice Baked Sweet Potatoes with Vegan Artichoke Cream Sauce	67
Yam Yums	68
Kale Chips	68

Fruits & Veggies On-the-Go	69
Dill Pickles	70
Gluten-Free Cornbread Stuffing	71
Cornbread	72
Healthy Baked Broccoli Tots	73

MAIN DISHES

Crispy Dulse Sandwich	74
Teriyaki Chicken and Vegetable Rice Bowl	75
Baked Potatoes and Vegetables	75
Chicken with Sun-dried Tomato Cream Sauce	76
Grilled Salmon with Mango Salsa	77
Mango Salsa	77
Vegetable Curry over Wild Rice	78
Curry Powder	78
Baked Stuffed Eggplant	79
Pasta Fajoli	80
Tomato Mushroom Stroganoff	81
Chicken Fajita Pasta	81
Pasta Primavera	82
Portobello Pasta	83
Wendy's Veggie Rigatoni	83-84
Vegetable Pasta	84
Mediterranean Salmon Pasta	85
Spaghetti Meat Mixture	86
Vegetable Lasagna	86
Marinara Sauce	87
Ratatouille	87
Stuffed Peppers	88
Meatloaf	89
Black Bean and Sweet Potato Burgers with Chipotle Sauce	90

Mexican Meat Mixture	91
Café Rio® Style Chicken	92
Café Rio® Beef	92
Fish Tacos	93
Vegetarian Enchiladas	94
Tacos	95
Alternative to Meat – Vegetable Mixture	96
Thai Lettuce Wraps	97
Taco Pita Pizza	98
Italian Pheasant	99
Mini Pizzas	100
Teriyaki Marinade	100
Taco Salad with Creamy Tomatillo Dressing	101
Grilled Garlic Shrimp over Marinated Veggie Rice	102
Pallela	103

SWEET BREADS & DESSERTS

Gluten-Free Chocolate Cupcakes or Muffins	104
Gluten-Free Banana Bread or Muffins	105
Gluten-Free Zucchini Bread	106
Gluten-Free Cranberry Orange Bread or Muffins	107
Coconut Pudding with Raspberry Sauce	108
Peaches and Cream-sicles	108
Raw Chocolate Chip Cookies	109
Resource Guide	110

WELCOME

Hi, I am Wendy P. Thueson, owner of Raw Chef Wendy™, LLC. Welcome to the first book of my RAWinspiring™ Recipe Series. I am so excited to be sharing this recipe book with you.

I began eating raw food in 2009 when I was in a desperate state of health. I had been suffering for years with many different symptoms, including debilitating neck and back pain, hypoglycemia, anemia, Grave's disease, infertility, brain fog, and even stuttering. My body was breaking down at only thirty-nine years old and I couldn't take the pain any longer. I was ready to take my life.

As I prayed one day in April, I begged God to get me out of my misery. I knew I couldn't do it on my own but I had no more hope that my life could be any different. As I lay there, barely able to move, I heard in my mind, "Wendy, it's not your time yet. Go to the computer and look up nutrition." I had been suspecting nutrition as being a big factor in why I was not feeling well. Having visited many doctors who ran test after test only for them to come back negative and wanting to prescribe me medicine and pain killers, I knew there had to be another way.

The day I asked my doctor what I could do nutritionally and he said to me, "I've heard the South Beach diet is a good one. Why don't you give that a try?" I was dumbfounded. How could someone who is supposed to be an expert at the human body not know a thing about nutrition? Walking out of his office that day, I committed to take my health into my own hands and figure this thing out on my own.

Researching nutrition, I came across raw food, a term I was not familiar with at the time. It was not mainstream like it is today, so I had to do some digging. I did find some books in the library and began my extensive research on nutrition and the ingredients and recipes available for me to try.

Having been to culinary school, I was familiar with many different ingredients and techniques of how to create delicious dishes, but the ingredients I was learning about in the raw food world were foreign to me: Irish moss, lucuma powder, maca, cacao. What where they? I learned -- after buying a lot of rare and expensive ingredients -- that these "superfoods" weren't really necessary to gain the nourishment and health I was looking for. I decided to keep things simple and cost-effective. I began playing around with other peoples' recipes that didn't taste so great, and creating my own with great flavors and textures that really satisfied.

I created the recipes in my new book, "Beautifully Raw"™ which is the second book in this series. People loved them when they tasted them in my classes but they didn't want to have to eat all raw foods. I noticed a huge gap from the Standard American Diet (S.A.D.) to eating the raw food lifestyle. I also noticed with my own experience, that when I changed my eating habits so drastically from eating meat every meal and drinking milk, eating eggs and cheese and very few vegetables or fruit to eating all fruits and vegetables and sprouted nuts and seeds, my body went into a bit of a shock. I also suffered from withdrawal symptoms from being a sugar addict. This sent me emotionally into places I wasn't prepared to go, as many emotions surfaced which I had been purposely shoving down with food to avoid.

I ended up asking for help emotionally from a friend who did emotional clearing, a healing modality that I believe is far more effective than talk therapy. This helped me tremendously and I was able to cope again. I tell you all of this because you may have some similar experiences happen to you. However, in writing this book and creating these recipes, I am handing you the bridge between these two worlds to help make your transition much smoother than what I experienced.

Many of these recipes are based on foods we are already used to eating like pizza, quiche, soups, salads, and of course, dessert. But I have 'healthified' the recipes by making most of the gluten-free, reducing the animal products like cheese, meat and dairy, and giving some alternatives to the highly processed sugary desserts we are so used to.

My hope is that you will try out each of these recipes and feed them to your family. Get them involved in preparing the food before meals and they will be more likely to want to try the foods you are preparing together with love.

As you eat healthier, reducing the amount of times you eat out and eat from packages this dead, processed stuff we call 'food,' I promise you will feel better. You may even begin losing weight, if needed, and you may notice some of the symptoms you've had go away. This is because these recipes having more nutrition than you may be used to and the way we cook them is different from traditional recipes. Pay attention to the 'helps' at the beginning of this book and do as the recipes suggest. This will help you have greater success in the long-run.

When I first started eating raw for my health, I had a negative mindset: I looked at all of the foods I could no longer eat and I felt deprived. I noticed I craved these foods even more because of the deep emotional tie I had to food. It helped me to change the way I was thinking about food by looking at all of the beautiful plant foods I could add to what I was eating rather than focusing on what I was subtracting. Being more positive changed my relationship with food for the better.

Whatever you decide, I highly encourage you to add more raw foods to your meals and eat a wide variety of plant-based foods that you and your family will love. I would also like to encourage you to keep in touch as you go through your raw food experience and ask for help when you need it. I am here to help support you in your efforts and help you succeed!
Visit www.rawchefwendy.com for more information.

May these recipes inspire you to eat healthier, resulting in greater energy and joy in life.

Reasonably Raw

After often being asked by my clients if they could just eat some raw foods and not "go all raw," I decided to put this recipe book together to help them transition over from the Standard American Diet (S.A.D) to a more healthy way of eating. I coined the phrase Reasonably Raw™ to help people understand that it is designed to go at their own pace. These and the Beautifully Raw™ Recipes in my RAWinspiring™ series are helping many people learn how to eat more fruits and vegetables and lower the heat when they cook so the enzymes will stay alive. This is important as these special plant enzymes help us with our digestion and all of the intricate functions of the body.

The human body has been designed to heal itself naturally. All we need to do is give it the food it needs for fuel, digestion, cleansing, nourishing and strengthening as well as repair and healing and it will do the rest. The problem, however, is that we have not been taught in this day and age to do that. We eat for pleasure and for pain.

I was one who would eat for momentary pleasure and then push myself toward pain. I was a sugar and carbohydrate addict and I couldn't stop at just one cookie or piece of cake. I ate until I started feeling sick. This is very typical of an alcoholic and I believe that many sugar addicts become alcoholics if they don't get things under control. I've also noticed that many alcoholics, when they become sober, go to sugar for a "fix." Sugar is as addictive as heroin, and grain products have an opioid effect on the brain, so we can actually feel high when we eat these foods. The problem is that we then crash from this euphoria and become exhausted, causing us to desire to repeat the cycle, which entrenches us deeper and deeper into the pleasure / pain trap.

The foods in this recipe book are designed to help you overcome those addictive behaviors, if you have them, and to help create an environment where your body can begin to heal itself with the delicious food you give it each day. You will notice that the dessert section is very small, which is done on purpose. If you feel like you need something sweet at the end of your meal, then you haven't had enough fruit throughout the day or at the beginning of the meal. Be sure to eat plenty of fruit so the cravings won't bother you anymore. If you are worried about high blood sugar, then read the book, "The 80/10/10 Diet" by Dr. Douglas N. Graham. He goes into depth about eating more fruit and keeping the fat low to help keep the sugars running through the bloodstream and not slowing down because of the fat. It will help you know how to eat better and not experience such highs and lows.

As you eat this way, spending a little time in the kitchen preparing the food, think positive, loving thoughts about your family and those for whom you are preparing it. The attitude of the cook is infused into the food and people can feel your energy and love or anger through it.

I used to hate cooking for my family because I felt no one appreciated it. This frustrated me to no end as I continued my "motherly duties" when my children were small. It seemed the kitchen was the only place I lived in most of the day because of the frequency in which everyone had to eat. We were eating often because we were filling our bodies with empty calories and never really feeling satisfied or full. We would stuff ourselves with food during a meal only to be hungry thirty minutes to an hour later. The dishes piled up and the daily chores seemed endless. In this state I was exhausted and resentful, which caused other problems with my relationships and beyond.

What I didn't realize at the time is that my feelings were infusing into the food and causing others around me to feel the same way I did. I look back on those days and we were all in survival mode, just barely getting by. Now that my children are older, we are not as stressed and I find myself spending less time in the kitchen. I love cooking again because I do it for enjoyment and because I love my family. Sometimes they take over and cook meals and they are now old enough that they can help with the load of jobs around the house. We are also eating much healthier as a family after seven years of my eating mostly raw foods and them adapting by eating more fruits and vegetables too.

I never force them to eat anything I make. I ask that they at least try one bite. I also ask that they take less than they think they can eat and if they want more, to add more after that. This helps cut down on waste of food and teaches them how to correctly portion their plates. We don't have as much waste as we used to and most of the food is compostable. The meat consumption in our family has gone down considerably. Now my children often ask if they can make fruit smoothies, salads and vegetable trays. They also love to fill a bowl with strawberries, bananas and berries for a snack. I have noticed the attitudes and behaviors have changed for the better and we are all enjoying one another more. We socialize around a tray of fruit or as we cut mangos instead of eating tons of bread, pastries, or cooked foods.

The power of one should never be underestimated. I have made a profound impact on my family, my community and the world at large by choosing to eat healthy and being a good example to others. I'm just getting started spreading this message, but I am so grateful for the impact I have had on others and the impact that others have had on me. We are all one in this way and we exchange energy, whether positive or negative. Why not create a positive impact on your family and community and the world as you make a conscious effort to eat healthier so you can look and feel amazing? It all begins with what you choose to put in your mouth each and every day.

Wendy P. Thueson
Owner of Raw Chef Wendy, LLC

Tips For Success

1. It is recommended that if you choose to eat animal products, purchase grass-fed beef, free-range organic chicken, wild fish (not farmed) and organic produce for best results. This is more expensive, which should also encourage you not to cook and eat as much. Just a taste or two is great for the flavor, but eating a lot more of the fruits and vegetables along with it is best for the greatest health benefits.

2. Any dish that has meat in it can be substituted with vegetables. Use the vegetable mixture recipe on page 96 to add a nice flavor without the meat.

3. Don't drink water with meals. Drink room temperature water up to 30 minutes before and 30 minutes after each meal. Cold water or drinks are hard on the liver and adding water to food dilutes the digestive juices, making it more difficult to digest your food.

4. If you have picky eaters, get them involved going shopping and cooking meals. When they help pick out the ingredients and prepare the meal, they are more likely to eat it.

5. Look at meal times as family bonding times. Guard this time as sacred. Plan schedules around your 3 meals each day, where possible, and sit down together with a positive attitude and love. Talk about happy, positive things instead of bringing up negative subjects or anger. These emotions are felt through your food, and the mood you create while eating also affects digestion. Infuse your food with love and those eating it will feel it too.

6. When going out to eat, choose dishes that have the most fruits and vegetables and very little meat. If the salad or meal has meat and you don't want to eat the portion they give, pick it off and ask if someone else wants it. I usually stick to restaurants with salad options, vegetable soups and Mexican dishes with plenty of lettuce, pico de gallo and guacamole. I love Café Rio and always order a large vegetarian salad so they give me double rice and black beans. I put plenty of lettuce, pico de gallo, guacamole, cilantro, limes, and ask for no tortilla, no corn chips and no cheese. I like their vinaigrette dressing. This is a filling and satisfying meal that I enjoy and it makes me feel great afterwards.

7. Stay away from processed sugar and avoid ordering or eating dessert after a meal. Also skip the sugary drinks. Sugar is as addictive as heroin and can cause problems with the eyes, heart, arteries, digestion, mind, and so much more. It makes the nerves in the body hyper and can cause severe damage over time. If you are addicted to sugar, choose fruit over dessert every time. Fruit sugar is different from processed sugar and your body needs this kind of sugar for fuel. Again, organic is best.

8. Cook meats first at medium high heat until cooked thoroughly. Reduce heat to low and add vegetables and spices last, including garlic and onions. Cover and simmer for up to two minutes, then remove from heat. You can tell if the plants have live enzymes if the vegetables are still bright in color and they have a slight crunch.

7 STEPS TO CONSCIOUS EATING

1. **STOP AND ASK YOURSELF QUESTIONS:**
    A. **What do I really want?**
        a. Fruit or vegetables
        b. Sugar - cake, donuts, candy, soda
        c. Bread (comfort)
        d. Chips, cheese (salt, fat)
    B. **Why do I want it?**
    Identify the emotion attached to the craving
    What is your motive or intention for eating it?
        a. Soothe or comfort
        b. Numb out or cover up
    C. **Will it move me toward pleasure or pain?**
    D. **What will it do to me afterward?**
    E. **Do I desire the consequences (good/bad)**
        b) If bad, why?
    F. **Is there something else that would benefit me more?**

All of these questions help you stop and think even before going into the kitchen. As you ask yourself these series of questions, you are becoming more conscious of your surroundings, your body, and what it wants vs. what it needs, and why you want the food or drink. Take a look at the list of 'What Cravings May Mean' below. Do you identify with any of these foods and possible feelings associated with them?

WHAT CRAVINGS MAY MEAN

Sugar ~ Desire for love or sweetness in life

Fat ~ Comfort

Salt ~ Desire relaxation and "to go with the flow"

Crunchy ~ Unexpressed anger, want attention

Spicy ~ Desire for intensity and action

Caffeine ~ Desire for control and calm in life

Bread and Soft Foods ~ Desire for comfort

Ice Cream ~ Desire for freedom and being carefree - like a child

Cheese ~ In need of nurturing

2. SLOW DOWN AND FOCUS ON THE PRESENT
   A. Make time for your meals and snack breaks.
   B. Schedule time around yourself, family and basic needs.
   C. Learn to say no and clear your schedule.
   D. Get rid of distractions (TV, video games, etc.).
   E. Focus on self-care every day. Make yourself a priority.
   F. Go out into nature and enjoy 20-30 minutes eating in the sunshine and savoring every bite.
   G. Close your eyes and enjoy the moment.

3. CREATE AN EXPERIENCE
   A. Be mindful when preparing food - infuse love into it.
   B. Set the table nicely to create a certain mood or theme to make it fun.
   C. Think positive thoughts about family and mealtime.
   D. Talk kindly to one another and keep conversation positive.
   E. Find healthier alternatives to traditional comfort food.
   F. Eat for energy and hunger instead of pleasure or pain.
   G. Ask for help with preparation and clean-up and enjoy bonding time over food. This helps relieve your stress and theirs too.

4. USE ALL 5 OF YOUR SENSES
   A. Create a sensual meal by using *sight* (presentation of food and beautiful colors), *smell* (inhale the smells before taking a bite), *taste* (notice where on the tongue the flavors are), *touch* (textures in the mouth), and *sound* (the crunch of the vegetables, for example).
   B. Slow down and savor every bite to create a sensual experience as you get in tune with your body and how food feels inside it.

5. POSITIVE INTENTION
If you are used to punishing yourself with food or numbing out, change your intention around food.

Look at healthy food in a new light: nourishing, energizing, strengthening, cleansing, healing, beautiful, safe, empowering and LOVE.

6. PRAY OVER YOUR MEAL
All of these things increase energy surrounding your eating experience but prayer is the most powerful in raising the vibration of the food.

7. GET OUT OF THE KITCHEN!
If your life seems to revolve around food, get out of the kitchen and find other things to focus on:

Hobby
Time with Family/Spouse
Take a Class

The Kitchen

THE KITCHEN

We all have different kitchens. Some of them are ideal to work in and others are not. Some are large and spacious and others are small and barely have room to store all we want them to. Whatever your circumstance, you can still make this work. Even if you are in a small apartment, there are ways to maximize your space. Trust me, I've done it!

I am laying it all out here so you can really get an understanding of how I began my Raw Food journey and learn from my mistakes, my challenges and my triumphs. I hope this helps you design your special place in your kitchen and create goals to help achieve the success you are searching for. This picture is of my kitchen. After 15 years, I decided to upgrade my cabinets by painting them white. It gave the room a beautiful, fresh new look and now I love going in there every day. I thought it would help you get a visual of what you can do with your kitchen, if desired. Play around with the space you have and create a sanctuary for preparing and eating your food.

Getting Real

Let's just get it all out on the table right now - my family and I are not perfect. We do not eat 100% raw and we have things in our kitchen that I would rather not have, but there are some battles I just don't want to fight.

Battling over food is not a good idea. People get very emotional over their food and if we try to control it, there can be disorders and other emotional side-effects to these behaviors. I suggest that you provide as much healthy food as possible and allow people to make their choices reasonably. An unreasonable choice would be to eat no fruits and vegetables and only animal products, breads and sweets. This, by the way, was a decision my 5-year-old made to rebel against me, and he paid for it by being backed up for two days and in a great deal of pain. Sometimes nature teaches the lessons a mom tries in vain to teach. He learned the hard way but it was a very effective lesson.

I allow my family to make their own choices and I am the best example I can be to them by eating what makes me feel healthy, energetic and happy. They see this in me and often ask if they can have what I am eating.

I taught my children young how to make salads, vegetable plates, green smoothies, and many more raw food dishes for snacks and meals. My hope is that they will take these good habits with them when they are ready to leave home and venture out on their own.

Some of my children aren't interested in learning how to cook very much. I continue to ask once in awhile if they'd like to help me make dinner or a snack. Sometimes they will and other times they won't. I figure they will come back some day and ask for lessons when they realize they ate better when they lived here than out on their own.

Decide how you want to handle meal times for your family. Getting children involved with the meal preparation is a sure way to get them to eat what you prepare together and try new things. Get them excited about the beautiful, colorful fruits and vegetables and teach them how to make basic recipes from this book. Create family bonding over healthy food to make healthier life-long choices.

STOCKING YOUR KITCHEN

When I first decided to eat raw food, I had to create a space that supported my new lifestyle. As I looked through my kitchen, the pantry, cupboard shelves, refrigerator, freezer and even food storage were full of junk foods, animal products and sugary processed snacks. Feeling overwhelmed, I didn't know where to begin. I wanted to just throw everything out, but it was hundreds of dollars' worth of food.

Re-evaluating my situation, I realized that I was the only one in the family who was determined to make this change. My family was not on board yet because they didn't have a compelling reason like I did. The harder I tried to convince them, the more they resisted. So I was on my own for a while and I needed my own cupboard to support my efforts. I also needed a plan.

I decided to work on myself first and not worry about anyone else. This is similar to the instructions given on an airplane when you are told to take the air mask and use it first, then help others. The realization hit me that I could not convince anyone else until the results I was looking for were achieved. This way I wouldn't have to convince them. They could see for themselves and if they wanted what I had, they could ask. That is exactly what happened. My kids and husband started asking for smoothies, salads and desserts I was making. It worked without me even having to try.

So find a cupboard or shelf you can have just for you and get started. Find some nice containers, if you can, and label them. I used clear ones with lids that fit close together to maximize the space. BPA-free is a good choice and glass containers with plastic lids are even better. You can find coupons for these in the newspaper, so watch for them.

Fruits and vegetables are the best if organic and non-GMO. I realize you may not be able to afford these at first, but please try and think more long-term. This is about prevention down the road. Less doctor visits, medications and sicknesses are often the results people receive from eating healthier. I visit the doctor once a year for a check-up and I am symptom and medication free.

You may also want to start a garden. You can grow an herb garden inside your home all year 'round and a seasonal garden in your yard. This will cut the food bill down quite a bit. It is also helpful to invest in a food dehydrator or freeze dryer to help preserve the food and their enzymes, which is better than canning at high heat. The items in these recipes should be raw - unroasted or uncooked and unsalted.

If you have allergies to any of these foods, choose foods like nuts or seeds that you do not have allergies to. There are always ways to substitute. Please do not feel like you have to purchase all of these items at once. You may add them gradually as needed with the recipes you choose.

The following pages are suggestions for what to stock in different areas in your kitchen. If you do not like something on the list or if you can think of other items, please - or + as needed.

THE COUNTER

I have a corner counter that is large where I put large bowls of a variety of fruits and it has my juicer and other tools to help support my raw lifestyle. Our family of 6 goes through the fruit in this corner in about 3 days. We keep it stocked because this is our medicine!

CUPBOARD OR PANTRY

- ☐ LEGUMES – Garbanzo beans, green split peas, yellow peas

- ☐ SEEDS – Sunflower seeds, sesame seeds, raw pumpkin seeds, chia seeds, hemp seeds, flax seeds, buckwheat, amaranth, millet, quinoa, gluten-free oat groats and rolled oats

- ☐ SPICES – Nutmeg, cinnamon, vanilla, cloves, Kirkland's Organic No-Salt Seasoning [Costco – I use this on a lot of things], cumin, parsley, basil, Italian spice blend, peppercorns, Real™ salt, sea salt or Himalayan salt

- ☐ SUPERFOODS – Cacao powder, cacao nibs, raw cacao butter, lucuma, maca powder, yacon powder, gogi berries, carob powder and other items you want to have on hand

- ☐ SWEETENERS – Organic coconut palm sugar, Medjool dates, organic raw honey

- ☐ OTHER – Raisins, dried cranberries, unsweetened coconut flakes, nutritional yeast

- ☐ FLOURS – Coconut flour, almond flour, my gluten-free flour blend

REFRIGERATOR

- ☐ VEGETABLES – Celery, carrots, bell peppers, leafy green lettuce, spinach, cucumbers, radishes, Spring mix and other vegetables you love

- ☐ NUT BUTTERS – Raw almond, cashew or other nut butters. *(I stay away from the peanut butters because of the aflatoxin mold they contain. Higher quality peanut butters contain much less of this mold than the cheaper brands. Always get Organic.)*

- ☐ SWEETENERS – Maple syrup

- ☐ SPICES – Garlic, onions, ginger root, turmeric

- ☐ LEFTOVERS – labeled and dated. Throw out after 7 days, if not eaten.

FREEZER

I keep these items in the freezer to last longer and keep them from going rancid. They are also raw – unroasted and unsalted.

- ☐ NUTS – Pecans, walnuts, cashews, macadamias, pine nuts, hazelnuts, almonds

- ☐ FROZEN FRUIT – Berries, fruit mix, peaches, etc.

ORGANIZATION

KITCHEN TRIANGLES

When I designed my kitchen, I read a book my mom gave me called, "Make Your House Do the Housework" by Don Aslett and Laura Aslett Simons that talked about the triangles of the kitchen. This is the most used pathway around your kitchen. For me the main triangle is the refrigerator, the island and the sink. The other areas like the stove and pantry are also a part of it, but this helps me to know where to put my zones.

ZONES

Creating zones in your kitchen will help you move around easier and know how to organize your cupboards and drawers to be more efficient. I have three main zones which create the first triangle called the **Food Prep Zone**. These are the areas of the kitchen that I move around in the most and consist of the **sink**, the **refrigerator**, and the **island**.

The next zone is the **Cooking Zone** which is comprised of the **stove**, the **refrigerator** and the **cupboards** above and below where I put spices, pots and pans, pasta and other cooking ingredients.

FOOD PREP ZONE

COOKING ZONE

BAKING ZONE

CLEANING ZONE

ZONES

The **Baking Zone** is next with the **pantry** shelves holding my flours, sugars and other baking ingredients, the small **counter-space** next to it - just above the dishwasher, and the **cupboard above** that area as well, which holds the baking spices and raw food ingredients. The island is also a part of this zone because I have cupboards and drawers below the island with baking equipment such as cookie sheets, measuring cups and spoons, spatulas, etc.

The final area is the **Cleaning Zone** which consists of the **sink**, a **cupboard** above for dishes, and the **dishwasher**. This zone is nice because I can do the dishes standing right there and reaching all of what I need to accomplish the task quickly.

If you think about what your needs are and what tools and appliances around the kitchen are needed for each task, you can create your zones accordingly and minimize the amount of time you have to go back and forth from one zone to another. This helps you prepare your food quicker and not be in other peoples' way when they come in and out of the kitchen. It also helps to organize your space and keep the clutter to a minimum. To learn more about zones and see my kitchen in a video, sign-up for my online program by visiting www.rawchefwendy.com where you can view the video in the bonus section.

NATURAL FRUIT & VEGETABLE WASH RECIPE

Yield: ~1 cup or small spray bottle
Ingredients:
1 Tablespoon fresh squeezed organic lemon juice or 3-5 drops lemon essential oil*
2 Tablespoons vinegar
1 cup distilled or pure water

Instructions:
Put all of these ingredients in a BPA-free spray bottle and shake before using. This can be sprayed on the fruit or vegetables and rubbed in a bit, then rinsed off (a much cheaper alternative to those bought in the store).

*I use Purify® essential oils because they are 100% organic and USDA certified. See Resource Section for more information.

Organization ~ 21

IDEAS TO INSPIRE

The following areas of my kitchen are ideas for you to possibly implement in your own kitchen if you desire or to get the creative juices flowing and inspire you to do your own thing. Whatever you choose, I suggest you create a space that helps you feel good about being in the kitchen and one that supports this new way of eating.

PANTRY
- I have changed over to healthier options for snacks. Cereal is one of those areas I have not demanded to be cut out completely because it is a fight I cannot win right now (even after 7+ years ~ I have rebellious teens in the house). My kids and husband rarely get the sugary kind and I try to find non-GMO cereals, but it can be a challenge. I have an organizer on the door for all of my odds and ends and I like to keep it clean and organized.
- I keep my small appliances like my Cuisinart food processor, rice cooker, Kitchen Aid stand mixer, crockpot, air popcorn maker and grain grinder along with my 5-gallon bucket of raw honey at the bottom of the pantry.
- On the second shelf I have the kids' dishes and glasses for easy access and some larger plastic containers for storage.
- On the third shelf I have the cereals and crackers, etc.

OTHER AREAS OF THE KITCHEN
- I have this cupboard next to the pantry on the left side of the sink, above the dishwasher. This is my designated zone in the kitchen for dishes to dry on the counter and for storing the following ingredients: baking spices, sugar substitutes, Blackstrap Plantain Molasses, and other items that I use for making raw desserts and gluten-free desserts on occasion. I also have gluten-free pasta and flours and some packaged gluten-free items.
- On the right side of my sink in the corner cupboard above the counter, I have my containers that are labeled with the seeds, Superfoods like maca, lucuma, gogi berries, etc. Dulse [seaweed], and other items I need for preparing my raw dishes. I also have larger bowls to mix with, my mandolin slicer and a few other small tools.
- In the cupboard below the same counter in the corner, I have my graduating glass bowls, cheese grater, nut & seed grinder [coffee grinder], and other small tools needed.
- In the thin cupboard on the left of the stove, I have my legumes and sprouting supplies, beans, seeds, etc. I also have my salt and pepper grinders, my protein shake, sprouted greens, other supplements and some Dr. Christopher herbal formulas for my children.

- To the right of the stove I have all of my spices and paper plates, plastic utensils, etc.
- In the island, I have my silverware drawer, knife drawer and other tool drawers. This is where I do most of my raw food preparation, bringing the items from the other cupboards, pantry and refrigerator together.
- I keep fruit roll-ups, homemade Green Smoothie roll-ups, dried fruit, raw nuts, granola bars, raisins and other snacks in the cupboard just above my fruit bowl that is always full in the corner.

FOOD PREPARATION TIPS

- When I prepare fruits and vegetables I like to have a large bowl available on the counter to put the peels and ends into which will go into my composter outside.
- The trash can and recycling should be handy for wrappers and other trash, although eating raw food really cuts down on the trash quite a bit.
- Having your knives and cutting boards handy and a wet towel or non-slip mat to go under it is always helpful so the board does not shift when you are cutting.
- I do not peel my fruit or vegetables, but on occasion I use a peeler to make my carved fruits and vegetables look good. I use a zester and other tools that are nice to have in one spot as well. These items and measuring cups, spoons, spatulas, knives, etc. are all in my island and are easily accessible when I need them.
- To clean off conventional fruit, you can use various products found in the grocery store, which often cause around $2.00+ for a small spray bottle full, or you can make your own [see recipe below].

Reasonably Raw Recipes

Recipes ~ 24

Beverages

WENDY'S GREEN SMOOTHIE

This smoothie is the first one I created that consistently tasted fabulous. I drink it just about every day. Work up to drinking a blender full throughout the morning, if possible.

Yield: 1 blender full
Ingredients:
4 large handfuls of fresh, leafy greens (kale, Spring mix, Swiss chard, spinach, etc. or a combination of these)
1 1/2 – 2 cups fresh fruit
1 cup ice
1 teaspoon chia seeds
1 Tablespoon flax seeds
1/2 – 2 cups water or fresh fruit juice

Instructions:
Blend in high-speed mixer and serve.

WENDY'S FALL GREEN SMOOTHIE

When I see apple cider and fresh cranberries in the store, I know it's time to make my favorite smoothie of all! I hope you love it just as much as I do.

Yield: 1 blender full
Ingredients:
2-3 large handfuls kale, Spring mix or other fresh mixed greens
3 cups fresh or frozen fruit blend
2 cups fresh cranberries
2-3 cups fresh apple cider
1 banana

Instructions:
Blend everything in a high speed blender and enjoy.

ORANGE JULIUS
Yield: 1 serving
Ingredients:
4 oranges, juiced
1 cup Almond Milk [recipe below]
2 cups ice
1-2 Tablespoons maple syrup
1 teaspoon vanilla
Dash cinnamon

Instructions:
In a high-speed blender, add all ingredients and blend until smooth.

WATERMELON SLUSHY
Yield: 4 servings
Ingredients:
4 cups fresh watermelon, cubed
2 cups ice

Instructions:
1. In a high-speed blender, blend together watermelon and ice until smooth.
2. Pour into cups and enjoy.

ALMOND MILK
Yield: 4 cups
Ingredients:
1 cup raw almonds
4 cups purified water

Instructions:
1. Blend almonds and water in a high-speed blender until smooth.
2. Strain mixture through a cheesecloth or a nut milk bag.
3. Do NOT throw away the almond meal. This can be used for any recipe with almond meal or flour in it.

*For a sweeter milk add 2-3 dates before blending and ½ teaspoon vanilla. Other nuts may be used like Brazil nuts that are high in selenium. Chestnuts or other nuts or seeds like hemp seeds may be substituted as well.

Breakfast

MUESLI
Yield: 8 servings
Ingredients:
4 cups raw rolled oats
2 cups mixed raw, unsalted pecans, pumpkin seeds and macadamia nuts or other nuts of your choice, soaked overnight and drained
1 cup coconut, shredded
1 teaspoon coconut oil
½ cup raw honey or organic maple syrup
1 cup each currants
1 cup raisins
1 cup dried cranberries
1 teaspoon cinnamon

Instructions:
1. Chop all nuts in processor until small chunks.
2. Mix all other ingredients together in a bowl with the nuts.
3. Spread on a Teflex® sheet and dehydrate 6-8 hours or overnight, until dry.
4. Can be kept in an airtight container in the cupboard for 1-2 weeks or the refrigerator or freezer up to 3 months.
5. Eat as a cereal with almond milk or use as a topping for dessert.

BAKED APPLE AND CRANBERRY OATMEAL
Yield: 9 servings
Ingredients:
2 cups rolled oats
2 cups Almond Milk [recipe on page 26] or water
½ teaspoon vanilla
½ cup slivered almonds
½ cup dried cranberries
1 large unpeeled apple
4 Tablespoons organic maple syrup
1 teaspoon cinnamon

Instructions:
1. Preheat oven to 350 F.
2. Prepare a large 3-quart baking dish and spray with oil.
3. Combine all ingredients in order in a large bowl. You may prepare this ahead the night before, just do not add the liquid until ready to bake.
4. Mix ingredients and pour into baking dish. Bake uncovered in oven for 1 hour.

ALMOST RAW GRANOLA BARS

I was on Pinterest and I saw a recipe for "healthy" granola bars. It had lots of sugar and other ingredients I would not consider healthy, like crispy rice. Did you know that most commercial crispy rice has corn syrup in it? I use the puffed rice instead; not raw, but healthier.

Yield: 4-6 bars
Ingredients:
1/4 cup raw honey
1/4 cup coconut oil
2 cups rolled oats, cut up a bit in the food processor
3 Medjool dates, pitted and chopped
1 cup organic puffed rice cereal
1/2 teaspoon vanilla
1/2 teaspoon cinnamon
Optional: 2 Tablespoons raisins, chopped, or use cacao nibs. You can also add raw almond butter for a peanut buttery flavor.

Instructions:
1. Mix all ingredients in a bowl, then transfer to a lightly greased loaf pan and press down firmly.
2. Refrigerate until firm.
3. Cut into rectangles and serve.
4. These are so good, you may need to double the recipe and divide for different mix-ins to create a variety of flavors.

HUEVOS RANCHEROS
Yield: 1 serving
Ingredients:
½ cup hash browns, cooked until lightly browned
1 egg, cooked with middle still runny
2 Tablespoons fresh salsa

Instructions:
On a plate, place ingredients as listed and enjoy.

CRUSTLESS QUICHE
Yield: 1 quiche or 8 servings
Ingredients:
5-6 eggs
1 cup milk or milk alternative
2 teaspoons Italian seasoning blend
2 teaspoons Kirkland's® Organic No-Salt Seasoning
1 ½ cups broccoli, cut
½ cup onion, diced
½ cup red peppers, diced
½ cup white cheddar cheese
Fresh parsley
Fresh basil
Olive oil

Instructions:
1. Preheat oven to 350 F.
2. In a medium bowl, crack eggs and whisk until yolks are liquid. Add milk and seasonings. Set aside.
3. In a pie plate, spray or wipe bottom and sides with olive oil. Add vegetables, herbs and cheese.
4. Pour egg and milk mixture over the vegetables and mix together gently with a fork.
5. Bake for about 45 minutes or until cooked through and browned on top.
6. Slice into 8 pieces and serve.

CRUSTLESS SPINACH QUICHE

Yield: 6 servings

Ingredients:

5 eggs
½ teaspoon Kirkland's® Organic No-Salt Seasoning
1 onion, chopped
2 large handfuls fresh spinach
½ cup mushrooms, diced small (optional)
1 cup shredded white cheddar cheese

Instructions:
1. Preheat oven to 350 F.
2. Spray or oil a pie plate and put onto a baking sheet. Set aside.
3. In a medium bowl, whisk together eggs and seasoning.
4. Add the onions, spinach, mushrooms and cheese into the pie plate and mix with a fork.
5. Pour egg mixture over vegetables and mix carefully together.
6. Place pie plate on baking sheet into the oven. Bake 30-40 minutes or until middle is set.
7. Cool for 5 minutes and cut into slices. Serve.

BREAKFAST EGG AND VEGETABLE MIXTURE & BREAKFAST BURRITOS

Yield: 4-6 servings

Ingredients:
½ onion, diced
1 red pepper, diced
1 cup fresh Portobello mushrooms, diced (other types of mushroom can be substituted)
1 clove garlic, minced
1 teaspoon Kirkland's® Organic No-Salt Seasoning
Dash ground pepper
5-6 eggs
2 Tablespoons water
½ cup white cheddar cheese, optional

Instructions:
1. In an oiled skillet, add all vegetables and spices and cook on low to medium heat for a few minutes until warmed but still brightly colored and crunchy.
2. In a medium bowl, crack eggs and whisk until yolks are liquid.
3. Add the eggs to the skillet with a tablespoon of water. Stir mixture until eggs are cooked through. Cheese may be added at the end if desired.
4. For breakfast burrito, take this mixture and place in the center vertically in a flour tortilla. Wrap up by folding over short ends at the end of the vegetable mixture and then roll from the sides into a burrito.

ORZO FRITATTA

Yield: 4 servings

Ingredients:
2 eggs
5 egg whites
1 teaspoon Kirkland's® Organic No-Salt Seasoning
1 teaspoon olive oil
1/2 cup mushrooms, thinly sliced (choose from shiitake, Portobello, or cremini)
1/2 cup red, orange or yellow bell pepper, diced
1/2 cup zucchini or yellow squash, diced
1 clove garlic, minced
1 cup gluten-free orzo pasta, cooked
2 Tablespoons green onions
1 teaspoon parsley, chopped
1 teaspoon basil, chopped

Instructions:
1. Cook orzo pasta according to directions.
2. Beat eggs and whites with No-Salt Seasoning in a bowl and set aside.
3. Heat olive oil in a skillet over medium heat. Add vegetables and sauté for about 2 minutes. Add garlic and onions and stir.
4. Add pasta and beaten egg mixture and stir until combined. Cook until eggs start to set and are lightly browned on bottom (4-5 minutes). Transfer skillet to oven on broil setting and lightly brown on top until eggs are cooked through.
5. Serve on a platter by transferring frittata with spatula. Garnish with fresh parsley or other herbs.

RAINBOW FRITTATA

Yield: 6 servings

Ingredients:

5 eggs
5 egg whites
1 red bell pepper, diced
½ yellow bell pepper, diced
½ orange bell pepper, diced
½ red onion, diced
1 ½ cups baby Portobello or shitake mushrooms, diced
½ cup shredded hash browns or diced and cooked potatoes with skins on
¼ cup shredded white cheddar cheese (optional)
2 Tablespoons extra-virgin olive oil
½ cup Almond Milk [recipe on page 26]
½ teaspoon Kirkland's® Organic No-Salt Seasoning
½ teaspoon Italian seasoning blend

Instructions:

1. Preheat oven to 350 F.
2. Add olive oil into a skillet and place in the oven.
3. In a large bowl, whisk eggs with milk, No-Salt Seasoning and Italian seasoning blend. Then add remaining ingredients to the bowl and lightly mix throughout.
4. Pour mixture into hot skillet and place back into the oven.
5. Cook for 25-35 minutes or until center is set, like a quiche.
6. Invert onto a serving plate or slice directly in pan.

Substitutions

EGG SUBSTITUTION
Yield: 1 egg
Ingredients:
1 Tablespoon flax seed meal
2 Tablespoons purified water

Instructions:
Place flax seed meal and water in a small bowl and mix together thoroughly. Let stand a couple of minutes while making a recipe. Add in place of 1 egg.

SUGAR SUBSTITUTIONS
Use these different ingredients in your recipes instead of processed sugar.

The following dry alternatives can be used cup for cup in place of sugar:
Coconut palm sugar
Organic raw sugar
Trehalose® – this is a natural sugar that the body makes (Wendy has a resource if you are interested in ordering some)
Medjool dates, pitted (do not use in cake recipes)

The following may be used but the liquid must be adjusted in a recipe (to adjust liquid in a recipe, use less liquid, for example: 1 cup water + 1 cup sugar = ¾ cup maple syrup + ¼ cup water):

Raw honey
Maple syrup

Date Paste: To make a date paste pit Medjool dates and add to a food processor. Process until mixture forms a ball. Slowly add water while machine is going until desired consistency is reached. This can be used in recipes to replace wet sweeteners cup for cup.

The following may be added whole to help sweeten a recipe like granola or cookies:
Raisins
Chopped dates
Currents
Dried cranberries, sweetened with fruit juice, not sugar
Cacao nibs
Carob nibs
Other dried fruits like bananas, mangos, apricots, etc.
Unsweetened coconut flakes

WENDY'S GLUTEN-FREE CAKE FLOUR MIX
Yield: 4 cups
Ingredients:
2 cups white rice flour
1 cup brown rice flour
½ cup potato starch
¼ cup tapioca flour
¼ cup arrowroot
2 ½ teaspoons guar gum
1 teaspoon pectin

Instructions:
1. Mix all ingredients together in a large bowl until thoroughly combined.
2. Store in an airtight container with a label and date.
   *Use for cakes, cupcakes, sweet breads, cookies, etc. anything without yeast.

BASIC RAW BREAD
Yield: About 24 pieces
Ingredients:
1 cup flax seeds, ground
1/3 cup flax seeds, whole
½ teaspoon sea salt
1 clove garlic, minced
2 Tablespoons onion, chopped
1 1/3 cups water
2/3 cup sunflower seeds, soaked 2 hours or more and rinsed
¼ cup black sesame seeds
1 teaspoon Italian seasoning
½ teaspoon Kirkland's® Organic No-Salt Seasoning

Instructions:
1. In a coffee grinder, grind the 1 cup flax seeds to a meal and place in a medium bowl.
2. Add the remaining ingredients and mix together well.
3. This will make chunky consistency bread. For smoother bread you may put in a food processor and process until smooth.
4. Put ½ the mixture on a Teflex® sheet which is on top of the mesh tray and spread to about ¼ of an inch thickness.
5. Dehydrate on 105 F. about 4 hours and turn over onto another Teflex® sheet.
6. Score into squares with a knife, being careful not to cut into the sheet, and dehydrate an additional hour.
7. Then remove from tray and use or put in a bag in the refrigerator.

Natural Yeast Breads

FEEDING NATURAL YEAST

With a dehydrated starter, add a few tablespoons water to create a paste. Then feed your start with 1 cup water and 1 heaping cup full of wheat flour. I like to use the Einkorn wheat if possible as this is not hybridized. The consistency should be a thick paste. Allow to sit out on the counter for a couple of hours, then cover and refrigerate for two days. Take from refrigerator and feed again, repeating the process above. After the second feeding, use up to 1 ½ cups of this start in recipes. Then feed again as before, repeating the process to create more. If you want larger batches, increase the amount of water and flour put in during the feedings.

If your starter sits longer than 5 days and begins to develop a dark-colored water on the top, drain the water and skim off any discoloration. Feed again and use in two days. This starter may be dehydrated -- when going on vacation or when you need to go longer in between feedings -- to avoid spoiling the starter. The longer you wait between feedings, the stronger the sour taste is in the bread.

NATURAL YEAST BREAD DOUGH

Yield: 1 loaf

Ingredients:
½ cup starter (stir before measuring)
2 ½ cups lukewarm water
1 Tablespoon olive oil
2 teaspoons salt
5 cups whole wheat flour
¼ cup roasted pumpkin seeds (optional)
½ cup roasted flax seeds, divided into ¼ cup portions (optional)
¼ cup roasted sunflower seeds (optional)

Instructions:
1. Mix first 5 ingredients in stand mixer, using dough hooks. Mix on medium-high for 5-7 minutes. Add seeds to dough and mix until thoroughly incorporated.
2. Place dough in greased bowl and cover with greased plastic wrap or heavy, damp kitchen towel. Allow to rise for 6-12 hours or until double in size.
3. Separate dough into two pieces and place each piece into a greased loaf pan.
4. Allow the dough to rise for 2- 2 ½ hours.
5. Bake for 35 minutes in a 350 F. oven.
6. Remove from pans and allow to cool completely.

Recipe is adapted from Beyond Basics with Natural Yeast by Melissa Richardson.

NATURAL YEAST PIZZA
Yield: 1 pizza
Ingredients:
1 recipe natural yeast pizza dough
1 recipe Marinara Sauce [recipe on page 87]
Toppings of your choice – suggestions: mozzarella cheese, pepperoni, olives, mushrooms, sweet peppers, artichoke hearts, sundried tomatoes, Kalamata olives, fresh herbs, pineapple, Canadian bacon, etc.

Instructions:
1. Preheat oven to 400 F.
2. Using your hands or a rolling pin, roll dough into a pizza crust ¼ inch thick.
3. Spread marinara sauce from the center of the pizza crust out to the edges.
4. Top with your favorite pizza toppings.
5. Bake for 15-17 minutes or until crust is golden brown.
    *For a crispier crust, before adding the marinara sauce and toppings, cook the crust for 5-7 minutes.

MULTI-GRAIN ROASTED FLAX AND PUMPKIN SEED LOAF

Yield: 1 loaf

Ingredients:
½ cup Starter (stir before measuring) [see recipe on page 36]
2 ½ cups lukewarm water
1 Tablespoon olive oil
2 teaspoons salt
5 cups whole wheat flour
¼ cup roasted pumpkin seeds (optional)
½ cup roasted flax seeds, divided into ¼ cup portions (optional)
¼ cup roasted sunflower seeds (optional)

Instructions:
1. Preheat oven to 350 F.
2. Mix first 5 ingredients in stand mixer, using dough hooks. Mix on medium-high for 5-7 minutes.
3. Add seeds to dough and mix until thoroughly incorporated.
4. Place dough in greased bowl and cover with greased plastic wrap or heavy, damp kitchen towel. Allow to rise for 6-12 hours or until double in size.
5. Separate dough into two pieces and place each piece into a greased loaf pan. Allow the dough to rise for 2- 2 ½ hours.
6. Bake for 35 minutes. Remove from pans and allow to cool completely.

Recipe is from <u>Beyond Basics with Natural Yeast</u> by Melissa Richardson.

STORING NATURAL YEAST

To store the natural yeast starter, refrigerate between use and be sure to feed every two days. Otherwise, you may dehydrate the starter by spreading it on a Teflex® sheet in a thin layer and dehydrating overnight until completely dry. Store in a sealable plastic bag with the name and date.

Soups

KALE & BUTTERNUT SQUASH SOUP

Yield: 8 cups

Ingredients:
2 cups butternut squash, peeled, seeded and cut into cubes
1 cup cooked wild rice
1 handful fresh kale, washed and torn into bite-size pieces
4-6 cups purified water or vegetable broth
1-2 teaspoons Kirkland's® Organic No-Salt Seasoning

Instructions:
1. Prepare wild rice according to directions.
2. Cut up butternut squash and kale.
3. In a soup pot, add the diced squash and water and warm on low heat until tender but not mushy, about 1 hour.
4. Add rice, kale and spices to pot and warm using your finger as a guide.
5. Serve immediately.

LENTIL SOUP

Yield: 10 servings

Ingredients:
8 cups vegetable broth
1 ½ cups very finely chopped onion
1 cup carrots, finely diced
1 cup celery, finely diced
3 cloves minced garlic
1 teaspoon olive oil
1 Tablespoon coconut palm sugar or raw honey
1 teaspoon dried basil, or more to taste (or 1 Tablespoon fresh basil)
1/4 cup chopped fresh parsley
1/2 teaspoon marjoram
1/2 teaspoon oregano
1/2 teaspoon thyme
1/2 teaspoon freshly ground black pepper

~ Ingredients continued on next page ~

1 teaspoon salt
1 bay leaf
2 cans tomatoes, diced (or 2 cups fresh tomatoes)
4 sun-dried tomatoes, reconstituted and diced
2 Tablespoons tomato paste
1/4 cup Braggs® Raw Apple Cider Vinegar
1 cup lentils
1 can (15-16 oz.) Great Northern beans

Additional ingredients to add at the end:
1 cup kale, diced into small pieces
Zucchini made into spaghetti noodles with a Spiralizer and chopped into ½ inch pieces.

Instructions:
1. Cook lentils in water until they are almost soft, about 35 minutes.
2. Drain and add remaining ingredients, except for the zucchini and kale, and simmer another 10-15 minutes on low heat.
3. Add the kale and warm for about 3 minutes.
4. Add the zucchini and simmer for 1 more minute. Serve.

WENDY'S VERSION OF ZUPPA TOSCANA
Yield: 6-8 servings
Ingredients:
3 cans (14 oz. each) vegetable broth
2 cups Almond Milk [recipe on page 26] or other nut milk
1 small onion, diced
Red pepper flakes (to taste)
Dash sea salt
Dash fresh ground pepper
1 Tablespoon nutritional yeast
2 Tablespoons sun-dried tomatoes, diced
4-5 cups chopped kale
1 Tablespoon Kirkland's® Organic No-Salt Seasoning
1 Tablespoon Italian seasoning blend
3 or 4 red potatoes, scrubbed and cut into slices or small chunks (skins left on)

Instructions:
1. Cook potatoes in a pot of water on low heat until tender, about 1 hour.
2. Rinse and drain potatoes.
3. Add remaining ingredients and warm about 20 minutes on low.
    *The original recipe has sausage and bacon crumbled on top.

WENDY'S VEGETARIAN VERSION OF WENDY'S® RESTAURANT CHILI

Yield: 6-8 servings

Ingredients:
1 (29 oz.) can tomato sauce
1 (29 oz.) can kidney beans with liquid
1 (29 oz.) can pinto beans with liquid
1 cup onion, diced (1 medium onion)
½ cup green chili, diced (2 fresh chilies)
¼ cup celery, diced
3 medium tomatoes, diced
2 teaspoons cumin powder
3 Tablespoons chili powder
1 ½ teaspoons ground pepper
½ Tablespoon Kirkland's® Organic No-Salt Seasoning
2 cups water

Instructions:
1. In a large pot, mix all ingredients.
2. Cook on low heat until warm.
   *For an even healthier version, soak and cook all the beans first and use fresh tomato sauce you make in your high-speed blender. Put in all vegetables at the end of cooking to retain the enzymes, and don't get it hotter than your finger can stand.

ZUCCHINI BASIL SOUP

Yield: 4-6 servings

Ingredients:
2 pounds zucchini, trimmed and cut crosswise into thirds
¾ cup onion, chopped
2 cloves garlic, minced
2 Tablespoons olive oil
3 cups water
1/3 cup packed basil leaves

Instructions:
1. In a food processor, chop up zucchini with skins on until small chunks.
2. Cook onion and garlic in the olive oil in a saucepan over medium-low heat, stirring constantly until softened, about 5 minutes.
3. Add water, then simmer partially covered until tender, about 15 minutes. Puree soup with basil in two batches in a blender. Be careful as this is very hot.
4. Pour into soup bowls and garnish with chopped basil and julienned zucchini if desired.

REFRIGERATOR SOUP

Yield: 4-6 servings

Ingredients:
1 cup lentils
2-3 large carrots, diced
2-3 cups red potatoes, diced
2-3 cups sweet potato, skinned and diced
*any other root vegetable of your choice
2-3 stalks celery, diced celery pieces
½ head cabbage, sliced and diced
½ large onion, diced
1 clove garlic, minced
1 can organic tomatoes
2 Tablespoons Better Than Bouillon® vegetable stock
1 Tablespoon Kirkland's® Organic No-Salt Seasoning
2 Tablespoons fresh parsley or 1 Tablespoon dried parsley
2 teaspoons Italian seasoning blend

Instructions:
1. Put 1 cup lentils in water. Allow to soak overnight or at least 6 hours. Rinse lentils until water runs clear.
2. In a small pot, boil 3 cups water. Turn off heat and add lentils. Cover until lentils turn soft.
3. In a large pot, fill until 2/3 full with purified water. Boil water, then turn off heat.
4. Add root vegetables and cover to cook until tender.
5. Add remaining ingredients and stir until combined.
6. Add lentils that have been cooked and drained.
7. Allow to simmer on low heat until all vegetables are tender but still have their color. (It's okay if they still have a slight crunch too. This means they still have some of their enzymes.)

Use whatever vegetables you have on hand: broccoli, zucchini or other squash, fresh tomatoes, etc. and dice into the same-sized pieces. Put harder vegetables in the pot first to become tender, then add softer vegetables after the root vegetables are soft.

MASSAMAN CURRY

An Indian-influenced dish that has become quite popular here in America. It is Wendy's husband's favorite Thai dish. This recipe has been adjusted to be much healthier but is not raw. It is, however, vegetarian and vegan.

Yield: 6 servings
Ingredients:
2 Tablespoons coconut palm sugar
½ Tablespoon sea salt
1 cup potatoes, peeled and cut into big cubes, 1" on all sides
2/3 cup onion, cut into big cubes the same size as potatoes
1 cup carrots, cut into same size as potatoes and onions
1 Tablespoon Massaman Curry Paste [recipe on page 44]
½ cup coconut milk
1 Tablespoon tamarind (optional)
1 cinnamon stick (optional)
¼ cup cashews (optional)
2 pinches cardamom (optional)
2 bay leaves (optional)

*Make this 1 day ahead and put in the refrigerator overnight to allow the flavors to infuse the vegetables.

Instructions:
1. Heat coconut milk with the Massaman Curry Paste in a pot over medium low heat. Break up the paste and mix well with the coconut milk. Stir constantly to keep the mixture from sticking.
2. After about 5 minutes, you should see the red oil bubbling up. Add the vegetables and stir to cover with the curry and milk mixture.
3. Add half a cup of water or enough to cover the vegetables. Stew for ½ hour or until vegetables are tender.
4. Let simmer for 20 minutes more and allow the liquid to be reduced so some of the chunks are visible and uncovered. Add a little more water if the liquid is too low.

MASSAMAN CURRY PASTE
Yield: Makes approximately 1 cup paste
Ingredients:
¼ cup raw peanuts, unsalted
2 shallots, sliced
5 cloves garlic, peeled
1-2 red chilies (or substitute 1/2 to 1 teaspoon dried crushed chili)
1 thumb-size piece ginger, thinly sliced
1 stalk lemongrass, minced (or 2-3 Tablespoons frozen or bottled, prepared lemongrass)
1 teaspoon ground coriander
½ Tablespoon ground cumin
½ teaspoon whole cumin seeds
1/8 teaspoon nutmeg
½ teaspoon cinnamon
1/8 teaspoon ground cloves
¼ teaspoon ground cardamom
2 Tablespoons fish sauce (optional but omit for vegetarian or vegan option)
1 teaspoon shrimp paste (optional but omit for vegetarian or vegan option)
1 teaspoon palm sugar
1-3 Tablespoons coconut milk, depending on how thick or runny you prefer your paste (save remainder for cooking your curry)

Instructions for Massaman Curry Paste:
1. Place all paste ingredients in a food processor (or blender) and process well.
2. To make a sauce rather than a paste, add up to 1 cup Thai coconut milk + ½ cup coconut meat.

*To store: Curry paste can be stored in a jar or other covered container in the refrigerator for up to 2 weeks; freeze thereafter. When ready to use, add coconut milk to make a sauce, then add your other ingredients.

POTATO SOUP

Yield: 8-10 servings
Ingredients:
6 slices thin turkey bacon, cut into 1-inch pieces (optional)
3 carrots, scrubbed clean and diced
3 stalks celery, diced
1 medium onion, diced
6 small russet potatoes, peeled and diced
1 Tablespoon olive oil
½ teaspoon Cajun spice mix (add more to taste)
1 teaspoon Kirkland's® Organic No-Salt Seasoning
8 cups low-sodium vegetable broth
1 cup Almond Milk [recipe on page 26]
3 Tablespoons all-purpose gluten-free flour or brown rice flour
½ cup coconut milk (fresh meat and water from a Thai coconut that is blended until smooth is best, but you may use from a can)
1 teaspoon minced fresh parsley
¼ cup grated cheddar cheese

Instructions:
1. Cook bacon and set aside.
2. In a large stock pot add carrots, celery, onion and potato with olive oil and cook over medium-low heat for about 5-7 minutes or until they start to get soft.
3. Season with spices then add the vegetable broth. Turn up the heat to medium and allow to come to a gentle boil.
4. After about 10 minutes, as the potatoes are becoming tender, whisk together the milk and flour in a small bowl and add to the soup mixture. Allow it to cook another 5 minutes.
5. Take out about ½ the soup and blend in a high-speed blender or food processor until smooth. Add back into the pot and mix with the remaining soup.
6. Allow to warm up again as you adjust for seasoning, adding a little more of any of the seasonings you feel it needs.
7. Add coconut milk and mix well.
8. Add fresh parsley and mix well.
9. Take off heat and pour into bowls. Top with a little cheddar cheese and a sprig of fresh parsley.

NEW ENGLAND CLAM CHOWDER
Yield: 8-10 servings
Ingredients:
3 strips turkey bacon, diced (optional)
5 cups potatoes, diced
1 medium leek or onion, diced
2 stalks celery, diced
2 cans (10 oz. each) clams, reserve juice
1 ½ cups chicken or vegetable broth
1 clove garlic, minced
Black pepper to taste
1-2 teaspoons Kirkland's® Organic No-Salt Seasoning
1-2 teaspoons parsley flakes
1 cup cream or whole milk or Almond Milk [recipe on page 26]
2 bay leaves

Instructions:
1. Boil potatoes until tender. Drain off liquid.
2. In same pan, cook diced turkey bacon.
3. Add onion, celery, garlic, and spices.
4. Return potatoes to pan; add clams and clam juice, broth, cream, and bay leaves.
5. Simmer on low heat for 30 minutes. Serve hot.

*This recipe is not like the Western "New England Clam Chowder" with a thick sauce.

TOSCANO SOUP
Yield: 8 servings
Ingredients:
2 teaspoons olive oil
2 medium onions, chopped
4 garlic cloves, minced
11 ¼ cups (90 ounces) vegetable broth
2 large tomatoes, diced
½ cup artichoke hearts + juice
2 cups coconut milk and meat blended in blender
Parmesan cheese or nutritional yeast
Fresh basil (if you only have dried, rub approximately 3/4 teaspoon between palms and add when you add the milk)
10 ounces baby spinach (fresh, half bag)

Instructions:
1. Add all ingredients except for the spinach, in order, into a large pot and heat until warm.
2. Stir in spinach just long enough to wilt.
3. Ladle into bowls and top with Parmesan cheese and fresh basil if you have it.

CHICKEN NOODLE SOUP

Yield: 6-8 servings
Ingredients:
Noodles:
6 eggs
1 cup olive oil
½ cup water
¾ teaspoon salt
4 cups Flour

Soup:
6 large carrots, sliced
1 celery stalk, diced
1 large onion, diced
1 ½ gallons chicken stock
4 lb. chicken breast, diced
Pepper to taste
Garlic to taste

Instructions for noodles:
1. Mix all noodle ingredients together.
2. Roll out in between two sheets of parchment or plastic wrap.
3. Cut into thin strips about ½ inch wide by ¼ inch thick.
4. Sprinkle corn meal or flour on top and mix the noodles around to prevent sticking.
5. Cook in boiling water with a dash of salt and 1 Tablespoon of extra virgin olive oil about 10-12 minutes or until noodles are done cooking. Drain.

Instructions for soup:
1. Bring all soup ingredients except diced chicken breast to boil.
2. Add chicken, pepper and garlic to taste.
3. Add noodles and boil 10 minutes.
4. Finish off with a bit of dried or fresh parsley.

GLUTEN-FREE EGG NOODLES
½ cup tapioca flour
½ cup arrowroot or non-GMO cornstarch
3 Tablespoons potato starch
¾ teaspoons sea salt
4 ½ teaspoons guar gum
3 large eggs or 4-5 egg whites
1 ½ Tablespoons extra virgin olive oil

Instructions for Gluten-Free Noodles
See instructions for regular noodles above. Use tapioca flour to flour the counter before rolling out.
Cook in boiling water 10-12 minutes. Drain and rinse well before serving.

VEGETABLE SOUP

Yield: 6-8 servings

Ingredients:
1 ½ cups lentils
5-6 large carrots, diced
4-5 large red potatoes, diced
1-2 Tablespoons olive oil
2 small zucchinis, diced
1 large leek, diced
3-4 large tomatoes, diced (or 1 can diced tomatoes)
1 Tablespoon garlic, minced
2-3 Tablespoons vegetable bullion
2 Tablespoons Kirkland's® Organic No-Salt Seasoning
1-2 Tablespoons Italian seasoning blend
1 teaspoon salt (regular or sea salt)
½ teaspoon ground pepper

Instructions:
1. In a small pot, add lentils with water to cover and then reduce heat to low until soft.
2. In a large pot, add carrots, potatoes, olive oil. Stir. Add 1 cup water if the mixture starts to stick to the bottom while cooking. Cook on medium heat until almost fork tender.
3. Add zucchini and leek, continue cooking about 5 minutes.
4. Add tomatoes, garlic, bullion, no-salt seasoning, Italian seasoning blend, salt, and pepper.
5. Add lentils and finish cooking on low heat another 5 minutes.
6. Serve warm with a green salad, fruit, and if you'd like, quesadillas or other bread.

CHICKEN TORTILLA SOUP
Yield: 8 servings
Ingredients:
2 Chicken breasts, whole, boneless, organic
1 Tablespoon olive oil
1 ½ teaspoons cumin
1 teaspoon chili powder
1 teaspoon Kirkland's® Organic No-Salt Seasoning
1 cup onion, diced
½ cup red bell pepper, diced
3 cloves garlic, minced
1 can (10 oz.) diced tomatoes (or 2-3 fresh tomatoes)
1 can (4 oz.) green chilies
4 cups low sodium chicken stock or vegetable stock
3 Tablespoons tomato paste
4 cups hot water
2 cans (15 oz. each) black beans, drained
3 Tablespoons cornmeal or masa
5 whole corn tortillas, cut into uniform strips about 2-3 inches

Optional Additions:
Sour cream
Black olives, sliced
Avocado, diced
Red or green onion, diced
Salsa or Pico de Gallo
Monterey Jack cheese, grated
Cilantro

Instructions:
1. Preheat oven to 350 F.
2. Mix spices together from cumin to no-salt seasoning. Drizzle olive oil onto chicken breasts and sprinkle about half the spice mixture evenly over the chicken breasts on both sides. Set remaining spice mixture aside.
3. On a baking pan that has been oiled or lined with parchment, place chicken breasts and bake for 30-35 minutes or until chicken is cooked in the center. Use two forks to shred the chicken when slightly cooled.
4. In a medium saucepan, mix together tomatoes, stock, tomato paste, water and black beans. Bring to a boil, then reduce heat to low and simmer.
5. Add the cornmeal with a small amount of water and pour into soup mixture, allowing it to simmer about 20 minutes longer. Taste to make sure seasonings are to your liking.
6. Add tortilla strips and gently stir in. Pour in bowls to serve after allowing to cool about 15 minutes and top with additions suggested or some of your own.

Salads & Dressings

CRAN-ORANGE QUINOA SALAD

Yield: 4 servings

Ingredients:
1 cup quinoa, cooked & cooled
½ white onion, chopped
½ English cucumber, diced
2 celery stalks, chopped
1 Gala or Granny Smith apple, chopped
3 Tablespoons raw pumpkin seeds
½ cup carrots, grated
1/8 cup dried cranberries

Dressing:
1 fresh squeezed orange juice
½ lemon
3 Tablespoons apple cider vinegar

Instructions:
1. Mix all ingredients together for the salad.
2. Mix all ingredients for dressing together.
3. Mix dressing into the salad.
4. Serve on top of mixed greens.

GREEK CRANBERRY SALAD

Yield: 8-10 servings

Ingredients:
2 heads lettuce, green leaf or spinach
½ cup dried cranberries
½ cup chopped pecans, soaked about 1 hour and rinsed
½ cup feta cheese (optional)
2 red apples, thinly sliced (or strawberries)

Dressing:
1 package Zesty Italian dressing (dry, made according to package directions)
1 teaspoon dry rosemary
1 teaspoon dry thyme
1 Tablespoon organic maple syrup

Instructions:
1. Make dressing and refrigerate at least 30 minutes.
2. Combine all ingredients for salad in order listed in a large bowl.
3. Dress salad and lightly toss together just before serving.

MEDITERRANEAN SALAD

Yield: 2-4 servings

Ingredients:

1 ½ cups boiling water
2/3 cup whole-wheat couscous or quinoa
1 teaspoon extra-virgin olive oil
1 fresh tomato, chopped
1 Tablespoon fresh parsley leaves, chopped
1 clove garlic, minced
1 Tablespoon capers (optional)
2 Tablespoons slivered almonds, toasted
Salt and pepper to taste

Instructions:

1. Pour boiling water over the couscous or quinoa in a mixing bowl.
2. Stir, cover, and let stand for 10 minutes.
3. With a fork, fluff the couscous, then stir in the olive oil and the other ingredients.
4. Add salt and pepper to taste. Serve at room temperature.

MEDITERRANEAN TUNA SALAD

Yield: 4 servings

Ingredients:

1 can (6 oz.) albacore tuna, packed in water, drained
2 Tablespoons red onion, finely chopped
¼ cup Kalamata or black olives, pitted and sliced
¼ cup crumbled feta cheese, optional
½ cup cherry tomatoes or diced tomatoes
½ avocado, diced
Juice of 1 lemon
Freshly ground black pepper
1 teaspoon Kirkland's® Organic No-Salt Seasoning
4 cups mixed greens

Instructions:

1. Combine tuna, onion, olives and feta cheese in a bowl.
2. Add lemon juice and spices. Mix well.
3. Serve over mixed greens and top with cherry tomatoes and avocado.

ARTICHOKE PASTA SALAD

Yield: 4 servings

Ingredients:
4 cups bowtie pasta, cooked and cooled
2 Tablespoons apple cider vinegar
3/4 cup cherry tomatoes, cut in half
¼ cup sun-dried tomatoes, chopped
2 Tablespoons fresh basil, chopped
1 Tablespoon fresh oregano, chopped
1 Tablespoon fresh parsley, chopped
1 teaspoon dried thyme
1 cup roasted organic chicken, cubed
1 cup marinated artichokes
3 Tablespoons marinade from artichokes in jar
Sea salt
Freshly ground black pepper

Instructions:
1. Toss all ingredients in a large bowl.
2. Refrigerate until ready to serve.
    *Excellent as a main dish over dark leafy greens or as a side. Fresh or roasted vegetables may be substituted for chicken or added if desired.

POMEGRANATE SALAD

Yield: 4-6 servings
Ingredients:
¼ cup slivered almonds
1 Tablespoon maple syrup
¼ teaspoon cinnamon
1 cup celery, chopped
3 green onions, sliced
1 cup fresh or 1 can (11 oz.) mandarin orange wedges
Pomegranate seeds

Dressing:
¼ cup grapeseed oil
2 Tablespoons vinegar
2 Tablespoons maple syrup or honey
1 Tablespoon fresh or dried parsley
½ teaspoon salt
Dash cayenne pepper
Dash ground black pepper

Ingredients:
1. Mix almonds, maple syrup and cinnamon together and dehydrate for 1 hour.
2. Mix all remaining ingredients together.
3. Add almonds and cover with dressing.

Dressing Instructions:
1. Combine all ingredients and mix well.
2. Serve over pomegranate salad.

SWEET POTATO SALAD BOWL
Yield: 1 serving
Ingredients:
1 cup brown or wild rice, cooked according to directions
1 sweet potato, baked and diced with skin on
½ cup roasted vegetables (I use my vegetable mix of sweet peppers, onions, mushrooms and garlic sautéed in a little olive oil)
¼ cup fresh parsley, chopped
Sea salt to taste
Ground pepper to taste

Instructions:
1. In a bowl, layer ingredients in the order listed.
2. Mix together lightly or serve as a layered salad in the bowl.

CAPRECE SUMMER SALAD
Yield: 4-6 servings
Ingredients:
Salad:
2 cups gluten-free small shell noodles, cooked
1 cup cantaloupe, cubed
½ cup grapes
1 green onion, diced
¼ cup raw cashews
2 Tablespoons red onions, minced

Dressing:
½ cup Vegenaise® non-soy mayonnaise
2 Medjool dates, pitted
1/8 teaspoon lemon juice
1/8 teaspoon powdered mustard
½ teaspoon chia seeds
½ clove garlic, minced

Instructions:
1. Put all salad ingredients in a bowl.
2. Make dressing in a separate bowl and pour over salad ingredients.

This recipe is a special one named after my friend Caprece who passed away. I talk more about her and how she influenced my life for good in my new book, RAWinspiring™

ROASTED GARLIC LEMON VINAIGRETTE
Yield: 1 cup
Ingredients:
¼ cup red wine vinegar
3 Tablespoons raw honey
½ teaspoon sea salt
1 Tablespoon roasted garlic (1 whole head of garlic)
3/4 cup extra-virgin olive oil
1/2 lemon, juiced

Instructions:
1. Sprinkle about 1 tablespoon olive oil over the whole head of garlic. Roast garlic over low heat just until the outside is slightly brown. This will help retain as much of the enzymes as possible.
2. Place vinegar, honey, salt and roasted garlic in a food processor. Puree until the garlic is chopped very fine.
3. With the food processor still running, add olive oil and lemon juice. Refrigerate until ready to use.

WARM BRUSSEL SPROUTS SALAD
Yield: 4-6 servings
Ingredients:
1 pound Brussels sprouts, stalks trimmed and dry outer leaves removed
1 clove garlic, minced
Juice of 1 lemon
¼ cup walnuts, soaked in water 6-8 hours, drained and chopped

Instructions:
1. Slice the Brussels sprouts with the slicing blade in a food processor or other method of choice into thin strips. Put into a skillet and add 2-3 Tablespoons water.
2. On low heat, warm the sprouts with the garlic, then add the remaining ingredients and serve immediately. This can be done with cabbage instead of Brussels sprouts as well.

THREE BEAN SALAD
Yield: 6 servings
Ingredients:
½ cup chickpeas, canned (or soaked, cooked and drained)
½ cup kidney beans, canned (or soaked, cooked and drained)
½ cup fresh green beans, cut into 1-inch slices
1 cup cucumber, diced
2 cups tomatoes, diced
½ cup red peppers, diced
1 cup sweet yellow or white onion, diced
2 Tablespoons apple cider vinegar
1 Tablespoon extra-virgin olive oil
2 Tablespoons fresh basil, chopped fine
1 Tablespoon fresh mint, chopped fine
1 Tablespoon fresh Italian parsley, chopped fine
Sea salt to taste
Ground pepper to taste

Instructions:
1. In a large bowl, combine beans, vegetables and spices.
2. Add vinegar, olive oil and salt and pepper. Toss to mix.
3. Let stand or refrigerate one hour before serving.

FRUIT SALAD WITH STRAWBERRY GINGER DRESSING
Yield: 4 servings
Ingredients:
1 cup strawberries, sliced
2 teaspoons maple syrup
Grated zest and juice of 1 lime
2 Tablespoons water (or more, as needed)
1 Tablespoon fresh ginger, finely chopped
2 peaches, chopped into ½ inch pieces (about 2 cups)
1 pint fresh blueberries
1 ½ cups mango, diced in ½-inch pieces
2 cups seedless watermelon, diced in ½-inch pieces
8 mint sprigs, chopped (optional)

Instructions:
Mix all ingredients in a large bowl and serve.

POTATO AND LENTIL SALAD

Yield: 4-6 servings

Ingredients:
2 cups lentils, cooked
1 cup potatoes, cooked and diced
½ cup green peas, lightly cooked
½ cup red bell pepper, chopped fine
¼ cup red onion, chopped
1 Tablespoon Italian parsley, chopped fine
2 Tablespoons apple cider vinegar
1 Tablespoon extra-virgin olive oil
Sea salt to taste
Ground pepper to taste

Instructions:
1. Combine vegetables in a bowl.
2. Whisk together oil and vinegar and add salt and pepper to taste in a separate bowl.
3. Combine oil and vinegar mixture with the lentil and potato mixture. Serve.

QUINOA, KALE & BUTTERNUT SQUASH SALAD

Yield: 4-6 servings

Ingredients:
2 cups kale, chopped (thick stems removed)
1 teaspoon extra virgin olive oil
2 cups quinoa
1 butternut squash, cooked and diced into small squares
4 Tablespoons slivered almonds
4 Tablespoons dried cranberries
3 Tablespoons raw apple cider vinegar
4 Tablespoons hemp hearts
1/8 cup red onion, diced
Sea salt and black pepper to taste
Juice of one orange or lemon
1 Tablespoon organic maple syrup
2 Tablespoons fresh parsley, chopped
1 teaspoon fresh rosemary or thyme, chopped

Instructions:
1. In a large bowl, massage the kale with 1 teaspoon of extra virgin olive oil and a pinch of salt until it softens.
2. Cook quinoa per package directions.
3. Drain, and pour quinoa over the chopped kale.
4. Add the remaining ingredients, and toss to combine.
5. Serve with lemon wedges, avocado slices, and hemp hearts if desired.

Snacks & Sides

CAFÉ-RIO® STYLE BLACK BEANS
Yield: 4-6 servings
Ingredients:
2 Tablespoons olive oil
2 cloves garlic, minced
1 teaspoon cumin
2 cans (15 oz. each) black beans
1 ½ cup of 100% tomato juice
½ teaspoon salt
2 Tablespoons chopped cilantro

Instructions:
1. In a large pot, sauté garlic and cumin in the olive oil for about 3-5 minutes or until a distinct aroma is created.
2. Add beans, tomato juice and salt and stir until everything is heated completely.
3. Keep warm until serving and right before serving, stir in cilantro.

ROASTED GARLIC POTATOES
Yield: 6-8 servings
Ingredients:
10-15 large red potatoes cut into quarters (or 20-30 small potatoes, cut in half)
¼ cup extra-virgin olive oil
2 teaspoons garlic, minced
1 teaspoons thyme (or 1 Tablespoon fresh thyme, chopped)
1 teaspoon dried parsley (or 2 Tablespoons fresh parsley, chopped)
1 teaspoon Kirkland's® No-Salt Seasoning

Instructions:
1. Preheat oven to 350 F.
2. In a 9"x13" baking dish, add potatoes and sprinkle with olive oil, garlic and spices.
3. Mix together and bake at 350 F. about 40 minutes or until lightly browned and soft when a fork is poked into a potato.

MEDITERRANEAN COUSCOUS

Couscous is a type of pasta that can be prepared in an instant. It is made from whole wheat, so if you have a wheat allergy, use quinoa instead, which is gluten-free. The couscous is done as soon as the 'grains' soak up the hot liquid. This recipe, with its traditional Mediterranean flavors, is a wonderful accompaniment to fish along with a salad of cucumbers, tomatoes and feta cheese if you like. Once you make this dish, you'll find yourself wanting to experiment with other flavorful additions to couscous or quinoa.

Yield: 2-4 servings
Ingredients:
1 ½ cups boiling water
2/3 cup whole-wheat couscous or quinoa
1 teaspoon extra-virgin olive oil
1 fresh tomato, chopped
1 Tablespoon fresh parsley leaves, chopped
1 clove garlic, minced
1 Tablespoon capers (optional)
2 Tablespoon slivered almonds, toasted
Salt and pepper to taste

Instructions:
1. Pour boiling water over the couscous or quinoa in a mixing bowl. Stir, cover, and let stand for 10 minutes.
2. Fluff the couscous with a fork, stir in the olive oil, then add the other ingredients.
3. Add salt and pepper to taste.
4. Serve at room temperature.

CHICKEN WALDORF SNACKERS

Yield: 6-8 servings
Instructions:
¼ cup Almondaise® - mayonnaise alternative with no soy
1 teaspoon fresh lemon juice
½ teaspoon maple syrup
¾ cup cooked chicken or turkey, diced
½ cup apple, diced
1/8 cup celery, diced
1/8 cup walnuts or pecans, soaked and chopped (optional)
About 24 gluten-free or whole grain crackers

Instructions:
1. In a medium bowl, combine Almondaise®, lemon juice and maple syrup.
2. Stir in remaining ingredients except for the crackers. Mix well.
3. Spoon ~1 tablespoon of mixture on each cracker and serve as a snack or hors d'oeuvre.

TOMATO & ZUCCHINI BAKE

Yield: 4 servings as side dish

Ingredients:
4-6 firm-ripe tomatoes, sliced ½ inch thick
1 medium zucchini, sliced ½ inch thick
Sea Salt
Freshly ground black pepper
2 Tablespoons fresh oregano leaves
1 Tablespoon fresh thyme leaves
1 cup feta cheese, crumbled or slices of mozzarella cheese

Instructions:
1. Preheat oven to 350 degrees F.
2. Lightly oil a 9"x13" baking sheet and alternate slices of tomato, zucchini and cheese until dish is full. Season with salt and pepper. Top with oregano and thyme leaves.
3. Place dish in oven and cook until slices soften a bit and cheese is melted, 10-15 minutes.
4. Serve as a side dish or as a main dish with a salad, vegetables and fruit.

CILANTRO LIME RICE
Yield: 4-6 servings
Ingredients:
1 cup uncooked white or brown rice
1 Tablespoon olive oil
1 teaspoon garlic, minced
2 teaspoons fresh squeezed lime juice
2 cups water or chicken broth
2 teaspoons chicken Better Than Bouillon® paste
3 Tablespoons fresh cilantro, chopped

Instructions:
1. In a saucepan combine rice, butter, garlic, 1 teaspoon lime juice, chicken broth and water. Bring to a boil. Cover and cook on low 15 minutes until rice is tender.
2. Remove from heat.
3. In a bowl combine remaining lime juice and chopped cilantro. Pour over hot cooked rice and mix in as you fluff the rice.

WARM ARTICHOKE DIP
Yield: 6-8 servings
Ingredients:
1 jar (12-14 oz.) artichoke hearts, drained and chopped
1 cup Parmesan cheese, grated
1 cup Almondaise® - mayonnaise alternative with no soy
1 tomato, chopped
1 bunch green onions, chopped

Instructions:
1. Preheat oven to 350 F.
2. Mix all ingredients together in the order they appear except tomato and green onions.
3. Pour mixture into an 8" x 8" glass baking dish and spread out.
4. Bake at 350 F. for 15-20 minutes or until lightly browned on top.
5. Sprinkle with tomato and onion and serve with crackers or vegetable sticks such as carrots, celery, cucumbers, etc.

MARGE'S NACHOS

Yield: 6 servings

Ingredients:
1 bag organic corn chips
1 can (15 oz.) black beans, drained
1 teaspoon garlic, minced
1 teaspoon cumin
Salt and pepper to taste
2-3 large tomatoes, chopped
1 can (6 oz.) black or Kalamata olives
1 avocado, diced
1 cup white cheddar cheese, shredded

Instructions:
1. On a large platter, spread out chips.
2. Add garlic, cumin, salt and pepper to black beans and mix well.
3. Spread beans over chips and continue layering ingredients as listed with the cheese on the top.
4. Bake on low broil until cheese melts.

NACHOS WITH WHITE SAUCE

Yield: 6 servings
Ingredients:
Alfredo Sauce:
3 Tablespoons butter or coconut oil
3 Tablespoons Wendy's gluten-free flour mix
1 Tablespoon vegetable or chicken bullion
1 cup milk or milk alternative
½ cup Parmesan cheese
1 teaspoons Kirkland's® Organic No-Salt Seasoning

Nachos:
Organic corn tortilla chips or fried wonton wrap strips
1 can (15 oz.) black beans
1 clove garlic, minced
1 teaspoon cumin
Salt and pepper to taste
1-2 large tomatoes, diced
¼ cup Kalamata olives
1-2 avocados, diced
1 cup white cheddar cheese
3 banana peppers
½ of a small red onion, diced

Instructions for Alfredo Sauce:
1. In a medium sauce pan, melt butter or coconut oil. Add gluten-free flour mix and stir to make a roux.
2. Add bullion and stir to incorporate.
3. Whisk in milk and keep stirring as the mixture thickens.
4. Add Parmesan cheese and no-salt seasoning. Mix well and take off heat.

Instructions:
1. Assemble ingredients with chips on the bottom.
2. Top with cheese.
3. Bake on low broil until cheese melts.

TORTILLA POCKETS
Yield: 2 servings
Ingredients:
2 large sprouted wheat tortillas or other gluten-free tortillas of your choice.

Filling of your choice: choose a few of the following ingredients and make your own.
½ cup hummus
½ cup wild rice
¼ cup fresh salsa
¼ cup pesto
¾ cup steamed vegetables (bell peppers, onions, mushrooms, zucchini or yellow squash)
½ cup black beans
½ cup cooked buckwheat, millet or quinoa
½ cup avocado
¾ cup fresh vegetables, grated
¼ cup sun-dried tomatoes
¼ cup soaked almonds, chopped
½ cup chicken, cooked or grilled
¼ cup cheese, grated

Also add fresh lettuce, tomatoes, Kalamata olives, or other fresh ingredients to complete these delicious tortilla pockets.

TWICE BAKED SWEET POTATOES WITH VEGAN ARTICHOKE CREAM SAUCE

Yield: 2 servings

Ingredients:
3 medium-sized sweet potatoes
3 cloves garlic
1 medium onion
1 Tablespoon olive oil
2 cups small sweet red peppers (or 1 large red pepper)
Handful of kale
1 Thai coconut (milk and meat blended together in blender)
Kirkland's® Organic No-Salt Seasoning

Artichoke Cream Sauce:
1/2 cup marinated artichoke hearts
1/3 cup fresh coconut milk or Almond Milk [recipe on page 26]
1 Tablespoon nutritional yeast
Bunch of cilantro
1 garlic clove, minced
Fresh juice of half a lemon
Water to thin out if needed

Instructions:
1. Preheat oven to 350 F.
2. Cut sweet potatoes in half and place on baking sheet facing down. Bake until soft when pierced with fork (approximately 45-50 minutes, depending on the size of the potatoes).
3. While potatoes are baking, mince garlic and chop onion. Add to pan with olive oil, and sauté for 5 minutes on low-medium heat. Chop peppers finely and add to pan, sauté for another 5 minutes or until peppers are slightly soft but still have their bright color.
4. Chop kale and add to pan for the last 2 minutes of cooking. Take pan off heat.
5. Take out potatoes from oven and let cool slightly.
6. Once cool enough to handle, scoop out potato flesh and place in large mixing bowl -- make sure to leave about 1/4 inch flesh around the skins.
7. Mash potatoes and add 1/3 cup coconut milk and stir well. Add salt and pepper and the sautéed veggies from the pan.
8. Scoop mixture back into potato skins and bake for another 8-10 minutes at 350 F degrees.
9. To make the sauce, combine all ingredients in a food processor and process until smooth (small chunks of artichoke will remain, which is fine). Pour over potatoes and enjoy!

YAM YUMS

Yield: 6-8 servings
Ingredients:
1 yam, peeled and chopped
1 teaspoon sea salt
1 ½- 2 Granny Smith apples, diced small
¼ cup organic maple syrup
1 ½ teaspoons cinnamon
1 Tablespoon coconut oil
½ cup soaked pecans (soak 20-30 minutes, until soft)

Instructions:
1. Mix yam and salt together and let sit 20-30 minutes to get moisture out.
2. Rinse salt off and place yams in saucepan and cover with water.
3. On lowest heat, simmer 30 minutes. Should be slightly soft but still have a crunch to them.
4. Drain. Add remaining ingredients.

KALE CHIPS

Yield: 4-6 servings
Ingredients:
2 bunches organic kale
1 cup cashews, soaked & drained
1 teaspoon Italian seasoning blend
½ teaspoon dill weed
1 teaspoon Kirkland's® Organic No-Salt Seasoning
½ teaspoon fresh garlic, minced
1 Tablespoon onion, minced
½- ¾ cup almond or hemp milk

Instructions:
1. Wash kale and let drain in a colander.
2. In a food processor, blend cashews until small chunks. Add remaining ingredients and pour milk in until mix has thinned out a bit. It still needs to be thick enough to stick to the leaves of the kale. The water on the kale will thin it a bit too.
3. In a large bowl, place the kale in and put the cashew mixture on top. With gloved hands, mix the two together until all leaves have been coated.
4. Place leaves in a thin layer onto dehydrator mats.
5. Dehydrate under 115 F degrees overnight or until all leaves are dry.
6. Store in a plastic container for up to several weeks (if you can).

FRUITS AND VEGGIES ON-THE-GO
Yield: 1 serving
Ingredients: Use any fruits or vegetables you desire or have on hand. These should be the center of your table and eat the fruit first as it digests the fastest. Eat plenty throughout the day. Some ideas are:

Vegetables: carrots with peels on, not the cut carrots already prepared from the store (these have been bleached), celery, cherry tomatoes, cucumbers, sweet peppers, broccoli, cauliflower, fresh beans, fresh sweet peas, etc.
Fruits: bananas, strawberries, blueberries, raspberries, blackberries, peaches, watermelon, honeydew melon, cantaloupe, kiwi, passion fruit, mangoes, pineapple, etc.

TIP: Squeeze a little lime juice on the melons or other fruit and enjoy another depth of delicious flavor!

DILL PICKLES
Yield: 1 quart jar
Ingredients:
4-6 pickling cucumbers
1 bay leaf
1 weed of dill
1-3 cloves of garlic, peeled
1 teaspoon dill seed
2 cups water
1 cup distilled vinegar
1 Tablespoon pickling salt

Instructions:
1. In a quart jar, place the bay leaf, dill weed, garlic and dill seed.
2. Combine water, vinegar and pickling salt in a saucepan and bring to a boil.
3. Scrub cucumbers and put in jar. Pour liquid mixture in the jar, leaving ¼ to ½ inch head space.
4. Wipe the top of the jar and put the lid on. Bring a water bath canner to a boil and process jars for 5 minutes.

GLUTEN-FREE CORNBREAD STUFFING

Yield: 6-8 servings

Ingredients:
2 cups onion, minced (approximately 1 medium sized onion)
2 cups celery, finely chopped
4 Tablespoons unsalted butter
8 cups toasted cornbread cubes [see Cornbread recipe on page 72]
1 teaspoon dried thyme
1 teaspoon ground sage
1 teaspoon Kirkland's® No-Salt Seasoning
¼ teaspoon ground black pepper
2 eggs
2 cups low sodium chicken broth

Instructions:
1. Preheat oven to 400 F.
2. Cut cornbread into ½ inch cubes. Split the cubes between 2 baking sheets and toast in a 400 F. oven for 10 minutes.
3. Lower temperature to 350 F.
4. Add all ingredients in order listed into a large bowl and mix together well.
5. In a 9" x 13" greased glass baking dish, spread mixture out evenly and bake for 25-30 minutes or until warm and lightly browned on top.

CORNBREAD

Yield: 8-9 servings

Ingredients:
1 cup gluten-free flour
1 cup yellow, white or blue cornmeal
2 to 4 Tablespoons sugar
1 Tablespoon baking powder
½ teaspoon salt
2 eggs
1 cup milk
¼ cup cooking oil or melted shortening

Instructions:
1. Preheat oven to 425 F.
2. In a mixing bowl stir together flour, cornmeal, sugar, baking powder and salt.
3. In another bowl beat together eggs, milk, and oil. Add to flour mixture and stir just until batter is smooth (do not overbeat).
4. Pour into a greased 9x9x2 inch baking pan. Bake at 425 F for 20 to 25 minutes or until golden brown.

HEALTHY BAKED BROCCOLI TOTS

Yield: 6-8 servings

Ingredients:
2 cups or 12 oz. uncooked frozen broccoli
1 large egg
¼ cup yellow onion, diced
1/3 cup white cheddar cheese
2/3 cup panko or finely ground gluten-free breadcrumbs
1 teaspoon Italian seasoning blend
2 Tablespoons dried parsley
½ teaspoon sea salt
½ teaspoon ground pepper

Instructions:
1. Preheat oven to 400 F.
2. Oil baking sheet with a thin layer of oil or line with parchment paper and set aside.
3. Blanch the broccoli in boiling water for 1 minute. Remove and place in ice bath to stop the cooking. Drain well.
4. Chop broccoli in food processor until fine, then add egg, onion, cheese, breadcrumbs and seasonings. Blend well.
5. Take about 1 ½ Tablespoons of mixture in your hands and gently press into a firm ball, then shape into a tater tot. Place on baking sheet and repeat the process with remaining mixture.
6. Bake until golden brown and crispy, about 18-24 minutes. Turn halfway through the baking process.
7. Remove from oven and enjoy with ketchup or other dip of your choice.

Main Dishes

CRISPY DULSE SANDWICH

This recipe is highly nutritious and very delicious! Dulse contains iodine and is excellent for thyroid health. I enjoy eating these sandwiches for lunch or dinner. It makes a great alternative to a BLT.

Yield: 2 servings
Ingredients:
2 Tablespoons coconut oil
Handful of Dulse (seaweed)
1 tomato, sliced thin
Green leaf lettuce, washed and in large pieces
Pickles – optional
Sunflower sprouts
1 avocado, mashed
Several squares of bread from the Basic Raw Bread [recipe on page 35] or gluten-free bread of your choice

Instructions:
1. Put the coconut oil in a small saucepan on medium heat.
2. When hot enough, but not too hot, put the dulse in the oil – piece by piece. It will swell up quickly.
3. Take the pieces out after only a few seconds of being in the oil and swelling, and place on the plate with the paper towel. Finish with all the dulse and set aside. Turn off heat.
4. On a piece of the Basic Raw Bread, spread the mashed avocado and arrange the rest of the toppings. Put the crispy dulse on last and another piece of bread. Serve. (I used gluten-free bread in the photo.)

TERIYAKI CHICKEN AND VEGETABLE RICE BOWL
Yield: 1 serving
Ingredients:
1 chicken breast, roasted or grilled with Teriyaki Marinade [recipe on 101], diced
1 ½ cups brown or wild rice
¾ cup grilled vegetable slices [vegetable mixture recipe on 97]
Extra marinade from cooked chicken

Instructions:
1. In a bowl, add ingredients as listed in layers.
2. Cook the extra marinade from the chicken. This can be done in a separate saucepan on the stove.
3. Pour extra marinade from the cooked chicken over the top and serve.

BAKED POTATOES AND VEGETABLES
Yield: 1 serving
Ingredients:
1 baked potato
½ cup Vegetable Mixture [recipe on page 96]
¼ cup cooked broccoli
3 Tablespoons fresh salsa

Instructions:
1. Cut open baked potato.
2. Add vegetable mixture, broccoli and salsa on top.
3. Enjoy!

CHICKEN WITH SUN-DRIED TOMATO CREAM SAUCE

Yield: 8 servings

Ingredients:

8 chicken thighs, bone-in, skin-on
3 Tablespoons butter, unsalted
1 cup chicken broth
1/2 cup Almond Milk [recipe on page 26]
1/4 cup Parmesan cheese (optional)
1/4 teaspoon basil, dried
1/4 cup basil leaves
3 cloves garlic
1/4 teaspoon oregano, dried
1/4 teaspoon thyme, dried
1 dash sea salt
1 dash freshly ground black pepper
1/4 teaspoon red pepper flakes
1/3 cup sun-dried tomatoes
White or brown rice

Instructions:

1. Cook chicken until done inside. Set aside.
2. In the same pan, make a roux with the butter.
3. Add chicken broth, milk and cheese (if desired) and whisk until it becomes a thick sauce.
4. Add remaining spices and ingredients and stir.
5. Cook rice as directed on package or potatoes until soft when pierced with a fork.
6. Serve the chicken over rice.

GRILLED SALMON WITH MANGO SALSA
Yield: 1 serving
Ingredients:
1 filet salmon with skin on
1 Tablespoon dill weed
Sea salt and ground pepper to taste
1 teaspoon Kirkland's® Organic No-Salt Seasoning

Instructions:
1. Season top of salmon with spices.
2. Grill on a pre-oiled grill on medium heat for 6-10 minutes, turning once during cooking.
3. Salmon filet should be light pink inside when cooked and not dry. Serve with a slice or two of lemon and mango salsa.

MANGO SALSA
Yield: 2 cups
Ingredients:
1 mango, peeled and diced
½ cup cucumber, peeled and diced
1 Tablespoon jalapeno pepper, seeded and finely chopped
½ cup red pepper, diced
1/3 cup red onion, diced
1 Tablespoon fresh lime juice
1 clove garlic, minced
1 teaspoon apple cider vinegar
½ teaspoon fresh ginger, minced
1 teaspoon maple syrup
¼ cup cilantro leaves, roughly chopped
Sea salt and ground pepper to taste

Instructions:
Mix all ingredients together in a bowl and serve with chips or over a main dish.

VEGETABLE CURRY OVER WILD RICE

Yield: 4-6 servings

Ingredients:

Curry Powder Recipe
½ teaspoon mustard seed powder
2 Tablespoons cumin seed powder
1 teaspoon coriander seed powder
¼ teaspoon cayenne powder
½ teaspoon turmeric powder
½ teaspoon ginger powder

Curry Instructions:
Mix all powders together and blend thoroughly. Store in airtight container with label and date.

Vegetable Curry Recipe
2 Tablespoons extra-virgin olive oil
1 large white or yellow onion, diced
2 cloves garlic, minced
1 Tablespoon fresh ginger, grated
1 cup fresh tomatoes, diced
1 cup carrots, diced
1 cup zucchini, diced
1 cup eggplant, diced
½ cup celery, diced
1 fresh Thai coconut milk and meat blended until smooth
2-3 Tablespoons curry blend, recipe above

Instructions:
1. Make curry blend and set aside.
2. In a large pot on medium-low heat, add olive oil, onions and garlic. Saute' for a couple of minutes.
3. Add vegetables, spices and coconut milk. Mix well and warm, then serve. The vegetables should still have a crunch and a bright color.

BAKED STUFFED EGGPLANT

Yield 4 servings

Ingredients:
2 small eggplants, about 8 ounces each
2 teaspoons extra-virgin olive oil
½ cup onion, chopped
½ cup red pepper, chopped
1 Tablespoons turkey bacon, diced
1 Tablespoon pine nuts or pecans, chopped
1 cup brown rice, cooked according to directions
1 tomato, diced
1 Tablespoon fresh Italian parsley, chopped fine
1 teaspoon Kirkland's® Organic No-Salt Seasoning
1 teaspoon Italian seasoning blend
1 teaspoon Parmesan cheese, grated

Instructions:
1. Preheat oven to 350 F.
2. Cut eggplants in half lengthwise. Score each side of eggplant at ½ inch intervals to create smaller cuts inside. Brush lightly with 1 teaspoon olive oil and place cut side down on baking sheet.
3. Bake until browned and eggplant is tender when pierced with skewer, about 15 minutes.
4. Reduce oven temperature to 325 F.
5. Meanwhile, combine onion and 1 teaspoon olive oil in large skillet. Cook, stirring until onion is tender, on medium heat, about 5 minutes.
6. Stir in the rice, tomato, turkey bacon, nuts and spices. Blend together and remove from heat.
7. With a spoon, remove eggplant flesh from each slice, leaving a ½ inch thick shell intact. Chop up the flesh and add to the rice mixture.
8. Pack rice mixture into eggplant shells. Sprinkle with Parmesan cheese and arrange on a parchment lined baking sheet.
9. Bake 20- 30 minutes at 350 F. uncovered until tops are lightly browned. Serve.

PASTA FAJOLI

Yield: 4-6 servings

Ingredients:
1 pound Portobello, Cremini, or Shiitake Mushrooms or a combination of each
1 small onion, diced
1 large carrot, julienned
3 stalks celery, chopped
2 cloves garlic, minced
3 cups tomatoes, diced
1 can (15 oz.) red kidney beans with liquid
1 can (15 oz.) great northern beans with liquid
1 can (12 oz.) vegetable juice like V8®
½ teaspoon Sea salt
1 teaspoon oregano or handful fresh
1 teaspoon basil or handful fresh
½ teaspoon pepper
½ teaspoon thyme
½ pound gluten-free Fajoli or other pasta

Instructions:
1. Sauté mushrooms, onion, carrot, celery and garlic for 10 minutes.
2. Combine tomatoes, kidney beans, great northern beans, vegetable juice and salt in saucepan. Simmer on low heat for 1 hour.
3. Add oregano, basil, pepper and thyme.
4. In separate pan cook pasta to boxed directions.
5. Cover with sauce and serve.

TOMATO MUSHROOM STROGANOFF
Yields: 4-6 servings
Ingredients:
1 pound steak, cut into ¼ inch strips or ground beef
1 Tablespoon olive oil for cooking steak
¼ cup apple cider vinegar
2 cups sliced fresh cremini or Portobello mushrooms
1 can (8 oz.) tomato sauce
½ cup sour cream
2 teaspoons Kirkland's® Organic No-Salt Seasoning
2-3 Tablespoons gluten-free flour or white rice flour
4 cups cooked, wide noodles (gluten-free if possible)

Instructions:
1. In a large skillet, brown steak until desired doneness and set aside.
2. Add vinegar and mushrooms to skillet; cook on medium low heat until liquid is almost evaporated.
3. Add tomato sauce and reserved beef. Bring to a boil; reduce heat, simmer 5 minutes.
4. Remove from heat. Gradually stir in sour cream. Serve over hot, cooked noodles.

CHICKEN FAJITA PASTA
Yield: 4-6 servings
Ingredients:
1 pound chicken breasts, boneless and skinless
1 Tablespoon olive oil
2 cups chicken broth, low-sodium or vegetable broth (I use Better Than Boullion® brand)
8 oz. penne pasta or gluten-free pasta, cooked
1/2 cup Almond Milk [recipe on page 26] or other milk alternative
3 cloves garlic
2 cups bell peppers, sliced into thin strips
2 cups onion, sliced into thin strips
½ cup sun-dried tomatoes, chopped
1 can (4 oz.) green chilies
1 envelope taco or fajita seasoning (check the label to be sure there is no MSG)

Instructions:
1. Cook chicken thoroughly and cut into cubes. Set aside.
2. Cook pasta according to package directions.
3. Using the same pan used for the chicken, sauté all vegetables for 1-2 minutes on low heat but keep the bright colors and crunch.
4. Add chicken broth and milk and stir, then add the spice packet and mix together.
5. Mix together with pasta and serve.

PASTA PRIMAVERA

Yield: 4-6 servings

Ingredients:
2 Tablespoons olive oil
1 clove garlic
1/8 cup yellow onion, diced
2-3 Tablespoons gluten-free flour or white rice flour
1-2 cups Almond Milk [recipe on page 26]
2 chicken breasts, cooked and diced (organic is best and this is optional; omit if you are vegetarian or vegan)
½ cup sun-dried tomatoes, diced
1/8 teaspoon fresh ground pepper
½ teaspoon ground thyme
1 teaspoon Kirkland's® Organic No-Salt Seasoning
3 Tablespoons Parmesan cheese
1 small jar artichoke hearts, drained
½ cup red, yellow or orange bell peppers or a combination of all three
¾ cup broccoli, chopped
Gluten-free bow-tie pasta or linguini pasta, cooked and drained

Instructions:
1. In a skillet, sauté onions and garlic in olive oil for 2-3 minutes on medium heat. Sprinkle in the flour and blend until combined.
2. Add milk and whisk until desired consistency is achieved. Add a little more if needed.
3. Add remaining ingredients, except pasta, and mix in until combined.
4. Serve over cooked pasta or gently combine pasta with sauce and serve.

PORTOBELLO PASTA
Yield: 4 servings
Ingredients:
1 Tablespoon olive oil
1 Tablespoon garlic, minced
½ pound Portobello mushrooms, cubed into bite-size pieces
1 red bell pepper, seeded and cubed
1 medium zucchini, sliced in ½ inch circles
¼ cup sun-dried tomatoes
1 Tablespoon red wine or balsamic vinegar
1 teaspoon Kirkland's® Organic No-Salt Seasoning
1 teaspoon Italian seasoning blend
1-lb. box gluten-free bow-tie pasta
Parmesan cheese, grated (optional)

Instructions:
1. Heat a pot of water to boiling.
2. In a non-stick skillet over medium heat, heat the oil. Sauté garlic, mushrooms, pepper and zucchini until soft; about 10 minutes. Stir often. Add vinegar.
3. Meanwhile, cook the pasta in boiling water and drain, reserving ½ cup of the pasta water.
4. In a large bowl, mix the pasta with the mushroom mixture. Add as much reserved pasta water as needed to moisten. Toss with Parmesan cheese.

Mushroom Selection and Storage: Look for dark-brown portobellos with strong stalks. Avoid those with dark gills. Store in a loosely-covered bowl in the refrigerator for up to two days.

Mushroom Preparation: Wipe with a damp paper towel to remove dirt. Remove stems and flavor broths with them. Do not overcook Portobello caps.

WENDY'S VEGGIE RIGATONI
Yield: 4 servings
Ingredients:
¾ cup olive oil
1 cup mushrooms, sliced
Sea salt and ground pepper to taste
2 teaspoons basil
¾ cup onion, chopped
¾ cup vegetable broth
2 ½ cups coconut milk and meat blended until liquid
3 cups mixture zucchini and yellow squash cut horizontally into chunks
¼ cup Parmesan cheese (or use pine nuts or nutritional yeast for a cheese-like taste for vegan option)

~ Instructions on next page ~

Instructions:
1. In a hot sauté pan add olive oil, mushrooms, basil, onion, sea salt and ground pepper and sauté on medium heat for approximately 60 to 90 seconds.
2. Add the broth and sauté for 60 seconds. Add the coconut milk/meat mixture and warm.
3. In 1 tablespoon olive oil, warm the zucchini and yellow squash pieces until just warm to the touch.
4. Pour the sauce over the squash pieces and add Parmesan cheese or pine nuts or a sprinkle of nutritional yeast and continue to toss until cheese is completely incorporated.
5. Transfer to plate, garnish with parsley.

GLUTEN-FREE VEGETABLE PASTA
Yield: 4-6 servings
Ingredients:
1 bag gluten-free penne pasta
2 Tablespoons olive oil
3 chicken breasts
2 yellow squash, diced
1/2 onion, diced
1 clove garlic
Sweet peas, diced
Small jar artichokes
2 Tablespoons sorghum flour
Almond Milk [recipe on page 26], about 2 cups
2 Tablespoons Olive Garden® dressing or Italian Dressing.

Instructions:
1. Boil pasta until 'al dente'. Meaning to the tooth or just soft. Rinse and set aside.
2. In a medium pot, add olive oil and chicken, cook until chicken is done. Dice and set aside.
3. In the same pot add to the juices of the chicken yellow squash, onion, garlic and sweet peas.
4. Cook on low heat until just tender.
5. Add jar of artichokes, juice reserved.
6. In the pot you made the pasta, add juice from the artichokes and sorghum flour. Whisk in almond milk.
7. Put everything into a medium pot, stir in dressing and serve.

MEDITERRANEAN SALMON PASTA

Yield: 4 servings

Ingredients:

2 cups uncooked multigrain or whole wheat penne pasta (16 oz.)
2 cups fresh broccoli florets
1 pound salmon cut into pieces
1 cup fresh mushrooms, sliced
2 cloves garlic, finely chopped
2 medium green onions, sliced
1 jar (8.5 oz.) sun-dried tomato halves, sliced or Julienne-cut, in oil
¼ cup fresh basil leaves, chopped
4 teaspoons non-GMO cornstarch or arrowroot
1 cup reduced-sodium chicken broth
½ cup crumbled feta cheese (optional)

Instructions:

1. Cook pasta without salt according to package directions
2. Add broccoli to the pasta during the last 3 minutes of cooking time. Drain.
3. Meanwhile, in a skillet, heat olive oil. Add salmon and sauté about 4 minutes, stirring frequently until salmon is tender. Remove from skillet.
4. Reduce heat to medium-low and in same skillet, cook and stir mushrooms and garlic for 2 minutes.
5. Stir in sun-dried tomatoes, onions and basil. Stir 1 minute longer.
6. In a 2 cup glass measuring cup, mix cornstarch and broth until smooth. Add to vegetable mixture in skillet, stir for 1 to 2 minutes or until sauce is thickened.
7. Stir in cooked pasta and salmon and stir until thoroughly combined. Sprinkle with feta cheese if desired.

SPAGHETTI MEAT MIXTURE

Yield: 4-6 servings

Ingredients:

½ pound grass fed ground beef (optional – you may just want a vegetarian option so leave this out)
½ onion, diced
1 clove garlic, minced
1 red bell pepper, diced
1 cup mushrooms (Portobello or cremini) – optional

Instructions:
1. In skillet, brown ground beef on medium heat until thoroughly cooked through.
2. Add remaining vegetables and reduce heat to medium low. Stir as they warm. Make sure they do not lose their color or crunch.
3. Add seasonings and mix well.
   *Serve over gluten-free pasta, spiralized zucchini noodles, or other noodles you enjoy. This is also great over lightly steamed vegetables.

VEGETABLE LASAGNA

Yield: 9 servings

Ingredients:

3 cups Marinara Sauce [recipe on page 87]
2-3 zucchini, cut lengthwise into thin noodle strips like lasagna
1 cup mushrooms (optional)
½ cup olives, sliced
1 bunch fresh parsley
1 cup mozzarella cheese, shredded
1-2 handfuls fresh spinach

Instructions:
1. Preheat oven to 350 F.
2. Spray or oil a 9"x13" baking dish. Spread 1 cup of the marinara sauce on the bottom, then layer zucchini noodles along the bottom.
3. Sprinkle ½ the mushrooms, 1/3 of the olives, 1/3 of the parsley and 1/3 of the cheese on top.
4. Repeat the layers with the middle layer made of spinach.
5. Finish with cheese, parsley and olives on top.
6. Bake in oven for about 20-30 minutes. Serve.

MARINARA SAUCE
Yield: 3 cups
Ingredients:
2 cups tomato sauce
1 cup tomato paste
1 Tablespoon Kirkland's® Organic No-Salt Seasoning
1 Tablespoon Italian seasoning blend

Instructions:
Blend in blender or whisk together until smooth.

RATATOUILLE
Yield: 6-8 servings
Ingredients:
1 eggplant, sliced in rounds
1-2 zucchini, sliced in rounds
1-2 cups mushrooms, sliced
1 onion, sliced
2-3 large tomatoes, chopped
3 cups marinara sauce [see recipe above]

Instructions:
1. Grease crockpot lightly with cooking spray or olive oil.
2. Spread the bottom of the crockpot with marinara sauce.
3. Layer zucchini, mushrooms, sliced onion, tomato and eggplant. Continue layering until all ingredients are gone.
4. Cook on low for 6 hours.

STUFFED PEPPERS

Yield: 4 servings

Ingredients:
1 can (14.5 oz.) vegetable broth
¼ cup quinoa, rinsed and drained
2 Tablespoons olive oil
½ cup onion, chopped (1 medium)
2 cloves garlic, minced
2 cups fresh mushrooms, diced
1 can (14.5 oz.) diced tomatoes, undrained
5 oz. fresh spinach, chopped
¼ teaspoon ground black pepper
½ cup Parmesan cheese
4 large sweet red peppers (or yellow or orange)

Instructions:
1. Preheat oven to 400 F.
2. In a medium saucepan bring broth to boil and stir in quinoa and return to boiling. Reduce heat and cook, covered, about 12 minutes or until tender. Drain, reserving cooking liquid.
3. In a large skillet heat oil over medium-high heat. Add onion and garlic and cook and stir for 30 seconds.
4. Add mushrooms and cook for 2 minutes or until just starting to get tender.
5. Stir in tomatoes, spinach and salt and pepper.
6. Add quinoa and rice mixture and ¼ the cheese. Stir to combine. Remove from heat.
7. Cut sweet peppers in half lengthwise; remove seeds and membranes.
8. Fill pepper halves with filling. Place peppers, filled side up in a 3-quart rectangular baking dish. Pour the reserved cooking liquid into dish around peppers.
9. Bake, covered, for 35 minutes. Sprinkle peppers with remaining cheese and bake, uncovered, about 10 minutes or until peppers are crisp and tender, with the peppers still a bright red color and the cheese is melted.

MEATLOAF

Yield: 1 loaf pan

Ingredients:
1 pound ground beef, grass fed or half beef and half ground turkey
1 Tablespoon flaxseed
2 Tablespoons water
1 Tablespoon parsley, chopped
1 Tablespoon sea salt
1 Tablespoon dried mustard
2 Tablespoons hemp seeds
1 Tablespoon Italian seasoning blend
1 clove garlic, chopped
1 cup oats
3 Tablespoons ketchup
1 Tablespoon Kirkland's® Organic No-Salt Seasoning
Ground pepper to taste
1 Tablespoon Worcestershire sauce

Optional vegetable add-ins:
½-1 cup each shredded carrots, zucchini, celery

Instructions:
1. Preheat oven to 350 F.
2. Mix all ingredients together.
3. Place mixture in loaf pan and spread evenly.
4. Bake at 350 degrees for 1 hour.

BLACK BEAN AND SWEET POTATO BURGERS WITH CHIPOTLE SAUCE

Yield: 6 burgers

Ingredients:
1 can (15 oz.) black beans, rinsed and drained well
1 medium baked or roasted sweet potato, peeled and mashed
½ cup cooked quinoa or brown rice
¼ cup ground flax seed meal
¼ cup red onion, finely chopped
1/8 cup cilantro, finely chopped
1/8 cup fresh parsley, finely chopped
¼ teaspoon cumin
1 teaspoon Kirkland's® Organic No-Salt Seasoning
Olive oil
½ cup Almondaise® (vegan mayonnaise)
½ teaspoon chipotle powder
1 large garlic clove, minced
1 Tablespoon fresh lime juice
Burger buns or large lettuce leaves
Avocado slices
Tomato slices
Dill pickle slices
Spring mix or arugula

Instructions:
1. Preheat grill to medium heat.
2. Combine beans and sweet potato in the bowl of a food processor. Blend together until mashed. Add quinoa, flax seed meal, onion, cilantro, parsley, cumin and no-salt seasoning, and pulse together until combined.
3. Form the mixture into 6 burgers with your hands. Brush both sides of each burger generously with olive oil and arrange on a grill basket. Grill 8-10 minutes on each side or until lightly browned.
4. Combine Almondaise®, chipotle powder, garlic and lime juice together in a small bowl.
5. Serve burgers on buns or in the large lettuce leaves. Add a dollop of the mayonnaise mixture and avocado, tomato, dill and arugula or Spring mix on top.

MEXICAN MEAT MIXTURE

Yield: 4 meals worth for a family of 4

Ingredients:
2-3 pounds ground grass-fed beef, cooked thoroughly and drained
2 cans (15.5 oz.) kidney beans
2 cans (14.5 oz.) diced tomatoes
1 can (4 oz.) green chilies
1 large red pepper, diced
1 onion, diced
2 teaspoons garlic, minced
2 Tablespoons cumin, ground
2 Tablespoons Kirkland's® Organic No-Salt Seasoning
3 Tablespoons taco seasoning

Instructions:
1. Brown ground beef until cooked thoroughly.
2. Turn heat to low and add canned ingredients.
3. Add vegetables and spices and stir together. Allow to heat through, then use some of the mixture for tacos, burritos or other Mexican dishes.
4. Allow remaining mix to cool completely and put in Ziplock® storage bags. Label and freeze.

CAFÉ RIO® STYLE CHICKEN
Yield: 2 pounds
Ingredients:
2 pounds chicken breasts
½ of a small bottle of zesty Italian dressing
½ Tablespoon garlic, minced
1 packet ranch dressing mix (mixed with ½ cup water)
½ Tablespoon chili powder
½ Tablespoon ground cumin

Instructions:
1. Place all ingredients in a crockpot.
2. Cook on high 5-6 hours or on low 8 hours.
3. Shred chicken with fork and serve in salads, burritos, tacos, etc.
   *You can also double or triple this to make extra for freezing. Then simply thaw and reheat for a quick meal.

CAFE RIO® STYLE BEEF
Yield: 10-12 servings
Ingredients:
3 pounds chuck roast
1 can (10 oz.) green chili enchilada sauce
1 cup beef broth
1 can (8 oz.) tomato sauce
1 Tablespoon cumin
½ onion
3 cloves of garlic, minced

Instructions
1. Place chuck roast in crockpot.
2. Pour green chili sauce, beef broth and tomato sauce over the top and add cumin and garlic.
3. Cut onion in half and place full onion rings on the top of the roast to flavor. They will be removed and discarded when the roast is cooked.
4. Cook on low for 8-9 hours, or until meat falls apart easily. Shred meat into a different container, strain juices from the crockpot and pour over shredded beef.

FISH TACOS

Yield: 8 servings

Ingredients:

Sauce:
1/3 cup Almondaise® or mayonnaise
1 Tablespoon Almond Milk [recipe on page 26]
½ teaspoon fresh lime juice

Pico de Gallo:
2 medium tomatoes, diced (about 1 ½ cups)
½ medium white onion, diced (about ¾ cup)
2 Tablespoons cilantro, chopped
1 teaspoon fresh lime juice
Dash sea salt
Dash ground black pepper
Dash cayenne pepper

Tacos:
Cooked fish filets or frozen fish sticks
Shredded cabbage
Small corn tortillas
Cilantro leaves as garnish
1 lime wedge per taco

Instructions:
1. Make the sauce by combining Almondaise®, milk and lime juice in a small bowl. Whisk until smooth, then cover and chill until needed.
2. Make salsa by combining ingredients in a medium bowl. Cover and chill.
3. Bake the frozen fish sticks as directed on the box. If not using the breaded sticks (gluten-free option) use un-breaded fish instead, cut into smaller strips for use as the filling.
4. Warm tortillas in the oven in a glass baking dish and place in a tortilla warmer.
5. Build each taco using two tortillas per taco. Drop a fish stick into the center of the tortillas, then spoon about 1 1/2 teaspoons of sauce over the fish. Add about 1/4 cup of cabbage and top off the taco with a couple spoons full of salsa. Serve with a lime wedge.

VEGETARIAN ENCHILADAS

Yield: 9 servings

Ingredients:
2 cups raw pumpkin seeds
3 yellow squash, diced
3 zucchini, diced
6 fresh Anaheim peppers, seeded and diced
1 Tablespoon cumin
2 teaspoons oregano
2 teaspoons garlic, minced
1 Tablespoon coriander, ground
Salt and ground pepper to taste
2 bunches of Cilantro
4 Tablespoons olive oil
2 cups vegetable broth
1 ½ cups corn
18 corn tortillas

Instructions:
1. Roast the pumpkin seeds in the oven on a cookie sheet until lightly toasted, about 2-3 minutes at 350 F.
2. In a food processor, grind up roasted pumpkin seeds. Set aside.
3. Dice onions and half of the Anaheim peppers. Sauté a couple of minutes in a medium pot with 2 tablespoons olive oil. Add spices and mix well.
4. Take pepper and onion mixture off the heat and add to the pumpkin seeds in the food processor, including the liquid. Blend until smooth.
5. In the same medium pot, add 2 tablespoons olive oil, then add the remaining diced Anaheim peppers, zucchini, onion, red peppers, vegetable broth and corn.
6. Warm corn tortillas.
7. In a 9x13 baking dish, spray or oil and layer of 6 corn tortillas on the bottom. Cover with 1/3 of the pumpkin mole' mixture, then layer 1/3 of the vegetable mixture and top with cheese, if desired.
8. Repeat the layers two more times, then bake in the oven for about 20 minutes or until cooked through and bubbly at 350 F.

TACOS

Yield: 2-4 servings
Ingredients:
Taco shells

Toppings:
Black bean mixture [recipe below]
White cheddar cheese, shredded (optional)
Olives
Lettuce or fresh herbs like parsley or cilantro
Fresh salsa or Pico de Gallo

Black bean mixture:
1 can (15 oz.) black beans
½ can (2 oz.) green chiles
1 tomato, diced
Taco seasoning
Cumin
Kirkland's® Organic No-Salt Seasoning

Instructions:
1. Mix together ingredients for the black bean mixture and warm on the stove until just warm to the touch. Remove from heat.
2. Take a taco shell and add a couple of spoonfuls of black bean mixture.
3. Then top with any of the remaining toppings you prefer.

ALTERNATIVE TO MEAT - VEGETABLE MIXTURE
Yield: 1-2 servings
Ingredients:
1 cup mushrooms, sliced
1 sweet bell pepper (red, yellow or orange), sliced
½ cup onion, sliced
1 teaspoon garlic, minced
1 teaspoon Kirkland's® Organic No-Salt Seasoning

Instructions:
1. Slice all vegetables thin and sauté in a pan with a Tablespoon olive oil or by themselves (no oil) and the pan covered with the lid.
2. Cook on medium heat a couple of minutes until warm but bright color is still visible and there is a slight crunch.
   *This meatless vegetable mixture may be used in place of meat in tacos or burritos with 1 teaspoon taco seasoning mix or in Italian dishes with 1 teaspoon Italian seasoning blend. Other flavors may also be added to create your own dish.

THAI LETTUCE WRAPS

This is the kind of recipe you will find in my Beautifully Raw recipe book. I'm adding it here so you can experience a little more of a raw food dish.

Yield: 4-6 servings
Ingredients:
Sauce:
2 Tablespoons Bragg's® Liquid Aminos or Raw Coconut Aminos
1 Tablespoon water
1 Tablespoon rice vinegar
1 Tablespoon sesame oil
1 Tablespoon natural peanut butter
1 Tablespoon raw honey
2 Tablespoon chili garlic sauce
2 cloves garlic

For 'chicken':
3 cups cashews or other nuts you prefer, soaked 1 hour to overnight, rinsed and drained
4 green onions, diced
1 can (8 oz.) water chestnuts, chopped
2 shallots, diced
Sea salt and ground pepper to taste
For Wraps:
1-2 heads Boston lettuce leaves, cleaned and dried

Instructions:
1. Mix all ingredients together for sauce.
2. In a skillet on low heat, add ingredients for 'chicken' mixture.
3. Pour sauce over the 'chicken' mixture and warm.
4. Place in a bowl with a spoon and serve with lettuce leaves. Put some of the 'chicken' mixture in the center of a leaf, fold like a taco, and enjoy!

Main Dishes ~ 97

TACO PITA PIZZA

Yield: 4-6 servings

Ingredients:
Pita bread
Vegetarian refried beans
Shredded cheese (if desired)
Fresh salsa
Olives
Red peppers
Lettuce

Instructions:
1. Preheat oven to 350 F.
2. Cover pita bread with refried beans, a little cheese (if desired) and bake in oven until warm.
3. Top with fresh salsa, olives, red peppers, and plenty of lettuce.
4. Cut into quarters and enjoy.

ITALIAN PHEASANT

Yield: 4-6 servings

Ingredients:
6 pheasant breasts
2 Tablespoons olive oil
1 Tablespoon Kirkland's Organic No-Salt Seasoning
Italian seasoning blend
1 cup onion, diced
1 teaspoon garlic, minced
3 stalks celery, diced
1 red pepper, diced
6-8 small artichoke hearts
6-8 sun-dried tomatoes
3 Tablespoons Olive Garden Salad Dressing
Sprinkle Parmesan Cheese

Instructions:
1. In large skillet, add olive oil and turn stove on to medium heat.
2. Add pheasant breasts and lightly brown on each side.
3. Sprinkle seasonings onto each side of the breasts while cooking.
4. Add remaining ingredients as listed except cheese.
5. Cook on low until breasts are juicy and tender and no longer pink inside with the lid on. Sprinkle parmesan cheese on top.
6. Turn off heat and allow to sit covered for about 5 minutes.
7. Serve over brown rice and add a salad and fruit tray.

MINI PIZZAS

Yield: 6-8 servings
Ingredients:
About 9 pieces of gluten-free bread or 1 package English muffins or pita bread, cut in halves and placed on a cookie sheet on parchment paper
1 small can (6 oz.) tomato paste
1 small can (8 oz.) tomato sauce
1 teaspoon Italian seasoning blend
1 teaspoon Kirkland's® Organic No-Salt Seasoning
1/2 garlic clove, minced
Mozzarella cheese
Cut vegetables like mushrooms, olives, peppers, sun-dried tomatoes, artichoke hearts, onions, etc.

Instructions:
1. Make sauce out of paste, sauce and seasonings.
2. Cover each piece with some cheese.
3. Add veggies.
4. Bake at 425 F. until bubbly, about 10 minutes.

TERIYAKI MARINADE

Yield: 1 cup
Ingredients:
½ cup Raw Coconut Aminos
¼ cup water
2 Tablespoons sweet rice wine
2 teaspoons coconut palm sugar
¼ cup organic raw honey or maple syrup
1 ½ teaspoon fresh garlic, minced
1 ½ teaspoon fresh ginger, minced
½ Tablespoon arrowroot

Instructions:
1. Mix all ingredients in a bowl and use as a marinade for meat or vegetables.
2. To thicken into a glaze, add ½ Tablespoon arrowroot or non-GMO cornstarch to cold marinade and warm on stove top in a pan until thickened.

TACO SALAD WITH CREAMY TOMATILLO DRESSING

Yield: 4 servings

Ingredients:

Dressing:
1 ½ cups cilantro (stems and leaves), chopped
1/3 cup coconut kefir or milk kefir
1 Tablespoon fresh lemon juice
2-3 tomatillos or green tomatoes
1 Tablespoon purified water
½ teaspoon ground cumin
¼ teaspoon salt, or to taste
¼ teaspoon freshly ground pepper, or to taste

Salad:
2 cans (15.5 oz. each) kidney or black beans, rinsed and drained
1 ½ cups fresh or frozen sweet corn kernels
½ red pepper, diced
¼ cup green onions, chopped
1 cup fresh tomatoes, chopped (about 2 medium)
1 avocado, peeled and diced
½ cup white cheddar cheese, shredded
¼ cup reduced-fat sour cream, (optional)
1 small jalapeno, seeded, deveined, and minced (optional)
½ cup blue corn tortilla chips, coarsely crushed

Instructions:
1. To prepare the dressing, add ingredients into a food processor and blend until smooth, about 30-60 seconds. Distribute dressing evenly between 4 quart wide-mouth mason jars.
2. To make the salad, distribute all ingredients evenly in layers between the 4 jars in the order they appear. If salads will not be eaten immediately, sprinkle lemon juice over the avocado pieces and mix gently before adding to jar. Chips may be put in a small bag to be added just before eating.
3. Place a lid on the top and store in the refrigerator up to three days. These are great as a lunch on-the-go or for dinner. Do not fill jar to the top. Allow some room to shake the jar to mix the contents before serving. Pour out onto a plate and eat with a fork.

GRILLED GARLIC SHRIMP OVER MARINATED VEGGIE RICE
Yield: 4 servings
Ingredients:
1 pound fresh or frozen shelled, uncooked large shrimp
2 cups water
1 cup long-grain brown or wild rice
1 cup broccoli, chopped in ¾ inch lengths
1 red bell pepper, cored and seeded, cut into ½ inch squares
1 medium zucchini, cut into bite-sized pieces
1 medium cucumber, diced
1 medium ripe tomato, finely chopped
¼ cup Teriyaki Marinade [recipe on page 100]
1 Tablespoon sesame seeds
3 Tablespoons rice vinegar
1 ½ teaspoon coconut palm sugar (optional)
1 ½ Tablespoons grated fresh ginger
¼ teaspoon Tabasco or cayenne pepper, or to taste
1 Tablespoon extra-virgin olive oil, plus additional for oiling the grill
1 Tablespoon garlic, minced
2 teaspoons raw honey
1 teaspoon Dijon mustard
1 bunch green onions, chopped
¼ cup carrots, shredded

Instructions:
1. Cook rice in 2 cups of water and bring to a boil in a saucepan. Cover and turn heat to low and simmer until all of the liquid is cooked in. Fluff the rice and remove from the heat.
2. Preheat grill to medium heat or use a stovetop to cook the shrimp just until pink but still tender.
3. Add sesame seeds, palm sugar, spices, olive oil, garlic, honey and mustard in a small bowl and mix well. Add shrimp to this mixture and coat.
4. In a medium bowl, add broccoli, pepper, zucchini, cucumber and tomato and mix together. Add marinade and toss to coat.
5. Place vegetables in a grill basket to grill until crisp but tender, about 3-5 minutes.
6. In a large bowl, add rice, vegetable mixture, shrimp with marinade, green onions and carrots. Mix together and serve on individual plates on a bed of dark leafy green lettuce.

PALLELA
Yield: 6-8 servings
Ingredients:
2 cups brown or wild rice, cooked
1 teaspoon garlic, minced
1 Tablespoon extra-virgin olive oil
1 small white or yellow onion, diced
1 large red pepper, diced
2 carrots, shredded
4 cups vegetable broth
2-3 bay leaves
1 teaspoon Kirkland's® Organic No-Salt Seasoning
2-3 large tomatoes, diced
1 teaspoon parsley
1 teaspoon Italian seasoning blend
Dash red pepper flakes or cayenne pepper
1 cup fresh or frozen green peas

Instructions:
1. In a large skillet over medium heat, add olive oil, garlic and onion and sauté for 1 minute.
2. Add pepper and carrots and cook another minute.
3. Add rice, peas and remaining spices and broth.
4. Mix well but not too much to make the mixture mushy. Warm and serve.

Baked Goods & Desserts

GLUTEN-FREE CHOCOLATE CUPCAKES OR MUFFINS
Yield: Two 8" round cake layers or 24 cupcakes
Ingredients:
2 cups Wendy's Gluten-Free Flour Blend [see page 35]
2 cups organic sugar or other dry sugar alternative
½ cup unsweetened cocoa powder
1 teaspoon baking powder
½ teaspoon baking soda
1 ½ cups milk or milk alternative
½ cup butter, coconut oil or vegan butter
1 teaspoon pure vanilla
2 eggs or egg replacer for a vegan option [egg substitution recipe on page 34]

Instructions:
1. In a bowl, combine flour, sugar, cocoa powder, baking powder and baking soda.
2. Add milk, butter and vanilla and beat with an electric mixer on low speed until combined.
3. Beat on high speed for 2 minutes.
4. Add eggs or egg replacer and beat 2 minutes more.
5. Pour into two greased 8" x 2" round pans or 24 cupcake liners.
6. Bake at 350 F. for 30-40 minutes or until toothpick comes out clean.
7. Leave in pan for 5 minutes.
8. Remove from pan onto a wire rack to cool completely.
9. May be frosted when cooled or eaten as muffins.
10. Store in refrigerator short-term or freezer for up to a month.

GLUTEN-FREE BANANA BREAD OR MUFFINS
Yield: 1 loaf
Ingredients:
1 ¾ cups Wendy's Gluten-Free Flour Mix [see page 35]
2/3 cup dry sugar alternative
2 teaspoons baking powder
½ teaspoon baking soda
¼ teaspoon salt
1 cup mashed ripe bananas (2-3 medium bananas)
1/3 cup butter, coconut oil or vegan butter
2 Tablespoon milk or milk alternative
2 eggs or egg alternative
¼ cup walnuts or pecans, chopped (optional)

Instructions:
1. In a large bowl, combine all dry ingredients.
2. Add banana, butter, milk, eggs and blend thoroughly.
3. Add nuts (optional) and stir in.
4. Pour into a loaf pan or 24 cupcake liners for muffins.
5. Bake at 350 F. for 55-60 minutes for the bread loaf or 30-40 minutes for muffins.
6. Allow to cool in pan 5 minutes, then turn over onto a wire rack to finish cooling completely.

GLUTEN-FREE ZUCCHINI BREAD

Yield: 1 loaf

Ingredients:

¼ cup chopped nuts (optional)
3 cups Wendy's Gluten-Free Flour Mix [see page 35]
1 teaspoon guar gum
1 cup organic sugar
2 teaspoons baking powder (aluminum free)
1 teaspoon cinnamon
½ teaspoon baking soda
¼ teaspoon sea salt
¾ cup butter (for a vegan option, use unsweetened applesauce)
2 eggs (for vegan option use 2 Tablespoons flaxseed meal + 4 Tablespoons water and mix)
2 teaspoons vanilla
2 cups fresh zucchini, shredded

Instructions:

1. Preheat oven to 350 F. and prepare a loaf pan by spraying with oil.
2. Mix all dry ingredients and whisk to combine. Set aside.
3. Melt butter (or use applesauce) and add eggs (or the flaxseed mixture) and vanilla and mix until combined.
4. Add wet ingredients to dry ingredients and mix until all flour is incorporated.
5. Pour batter into prepared loaf pan and bake 1 hour or until toothpick inserted comes out clean.
6. Cool in pan 5 minutes then invert onto a cooling rack until completely cool.

GLUTEN-FREE CRANBERRY ORANGE BREAD OR MUFFINS

Yield: 1 loaf or 24 muffins

Ingredients:

½ cup butter (or applesauce for vegan version)
1 cup organic sugar (or 1 cup date paste for no-sugar alternative)
2 eggs (or 2 Tablespoons flaxseed meal + 4 Tablespoons water, mixed, for vegan version)
½ cup Almond Milk [recipe on page 26]
2 cups Wendy's Gluten-Free Flour Mix [see page 35]
2 teaspoons baking powder
1 teaspoon guar gum
½ teaspoon sea salt
1 cup fresh or frozen cranberries, coarsely chopped
1 ½ teaspoons grated orange peel
1 Tablespoon fresh orange juice
½ cup pecans, coarsely chopped (optional)

Orange Glaze:
1 cup powdered sugar
1 Tablespoon + 1 teaspoon orange juice

Instructions:

1. Preheat oven to 375 F.
2. Cream butter and sugar or vegan alternatives together.
3. Beat in eggs or flaxseed mixture and add milk.
4. Combine flour, baking powder and salt. Add to butter mixture; stir just until moistened.
5. Fold cranberries, orange peel, and pecans into batter.
6. Grease and flour loaf pan and pour batter into pan. Bake for 25-35 minutes or until toothpick comes out clean.
7. Cool in loaf pan 5 minutes, then invert onto baking rack.
8. Finish cooling, then stripe glaze on top in a fun pattern.

COCONUT PUDDING WITH RASPBERRY SAUCE
Yield: 2 cups
Ingredients:
1 cup shredded coconut, no sugar
1 cup Almond Milk [recipe on page 26]
1 teaspoon vanilla
1 Tablespoon organic maple syrup
2 Tablespoons water
1 Tablespoon cornstarch

Raspberry Sauce:
1 cup fresh raspberries
1 Tablespoon organic maple syrup

Instructions:
1. In a saucepan mix coconut, milk, vanilla and maple syrup. Heat until hot throughout.
2. Meanwhile, mix cornstarch and water to make a slurry. Add to hot mixture.
3. Refrigerate overnight.
4. Mix raspberries and maple syrup together.
5. Serve pudding in parfait glasses and top with raspberry mixture.

PEACHES AND CREAM-SICLES
Yield: 6 frozen pops
Ingredients:
8 very ripe peaches
½ cup Medjool dates, pitted
1 cup fresh Thai coconut milk & meat blended together
1 cup Almond Milk [recipe on page 26]

Instructions:
1. Pit peaches and combine with dates, coconut milk and meat, and add almond milk. Blend until smooth.
2. Pour mixture into popsicle molds and freeze 3-4 hours, or overnight.

RAW CHOCOLATE CHIP COOKIES
Yield: 2 dozen cookies
Ingredients:
2 cups raw rolled oats
1 cup shredded coconut, unsweetened
¼ cup cacao nibs
½ cup dried cranberries or raisins – optional
4 Medjool dates, pitted and diced small
1 teaspoon flaxseed meal
1 teaspoon cinnamon
¾ cup coconut oil
½ cup raw almond butter
¼ - ½ cup raw honey, depending on how sweet you want them.
1 Tablespoon vanilla
1 pinch each Sea salt and cayenne pepper

Instructions:
1. Soak the cacao nibs in water at least 10-20 minutes to soften.
2. Mix all dry ingredients in a medium bowl.
3. Mix all wet ingredients in a small bowl.
4. Add wet ingredients to dry ingredients and mix well. If smaller chunks are desired, pulse in a food processor a few times.
5. Form balls with a spoon or ice cream scoop and place on a parchment lined baking sheet.
6. Freeze for 15 minutes or until firm.
7. These may be stored in the refrigerator or freezer up to 3 months.

RESOURCE GUIDE

I have been searching high and low the past 5+ years for help with various issues I have dealt with. I understand that our food, even the organic kind, is not grown in rich, nutrient dense soil and we have become deficient. We do the best we can with organic foods, but I found that I was still deficient in some areas. The following are resources for you if you feel you need them. They are companies and products that I have used and I love. I feel confident in recommending them because they have worked for me. If you have any questions about them or how to order them, please contact me at RawChefWendy@gmail.com

ESSENTIAL OILS ** There are many essential oils companies out there, but the quality varies greatly. The #1 word you need to see on the label is ORGANIC. If it doesn't say Certified Organic, then it isn't. The essential oils are the life blood of the plant and they are a very concentrated form - up to 100 times! The body utilizes the essential oils immediately and it uptakes all of the extras like pesticides, toxins and sewage sludge with it, if it is NOT Certified Organic or Wild Crafted (even better than organic because they are not farmed, but taken from the wild where the plants have not been sprayed and they are in their natural environment).

I recommend the essential oils from Purify Skin Therapy®. They are Certified Organic and Wild Crafted and are sourced by Holly Draper, the only Medical Aroma Therapist in the State of Utah. She is highly educated on the safety, use and efficacy of essential oils. After using essential oils from upwards of 6 different companies, these are the only ones I will use. You can order them at great prices from this link: http://www.purifyskintherapy.com/?Click=286

WARNING: Many companies teach that it is fine to put essential oils on infants and children of all ages. Holly teaches that Peppermint essential oil can suffocate an infant and cause them to stop breathing. DO NOT USE PEPPERMINT ON A CHILD UNDER 3 YEARS OF AGE! To adjust the mint recipe for a small child, please just use the mint leaves. You may use a few more to get the desired taste, but do not use the oil. Educate your family and friends about this danger and please come to Holly's classes to learn more or visit her website at the link above.

*Wendy does receive a very small affiliate bonus when you use the links provided in the resource section.

RECOMMENDED SUPPLEMENTATION

When I first began eating, I was a sugar addict and was attempting to get off of processed foods, so I naturally replaced the sugar with fruit. The problem was, I also had a yeast overgrowth, or Candida. This was very uncomfortable for me and difficult to control. If you don't know what this is or the symptoms associated with it, they can be as follows:

FOR MEN: Athlete's foot, fungus in fingernails and toenails, jock itch, etc.
FOR WOMEN: Fungus in fingernails and toenails, vaginal itching and discharge anywhere from a thin, yellow color to a thick, cottage cheese appearance.

These and other symptoms can occur when the body is out of pH balance. This has to do with the amount of acid or alkalinity we have in our system. We need a more alkaline than acid environment: 7.2 on the pH scale is about neutral. The more acidic we are, the more prone to sickness and disease we become. Colds and flu are a bit more acidic and cancer is very acidic.

This has a great deal to do with what we eat and it can be difficult to achieve a consistent balance with food alone. That is why I highly recommend the Purium® products. They are great for supplementation for nutrition that we are lacking and to help keep the pH balanced. Because of the pesticides, hormones, lack of nutrients in the soil and toxins in the air and water, we need some help to maintain balance.

After being approached by multiple companies and trying hundreds of products from the store shelves and other companies, I have chosen a company with the highest quality products I can find. They are certified organic, non-GMO, raw, soy-free, gluten-free, and are delicious. I consider these concentrated nutrients that can replace some meals. The greens are sprouted and have a very impressive amount of nutrients. I put these together with a banana in my shakes in the morning.

To learn more about the products and the company, visit:
mypurium.com/rawchefwendy

$50 Gift Card
If this is the first time you have been introduced to Purium®, please use the gift card code: *rawchefwendy* to receive your first $50 off; otherwise, use the gift card code given to you by your friend who introduced it to you.

For a list of books I recommend, please visit:
http://astore.amazon.com/rawchefwendyc-20

For a list of equipment I recommend, please visit:
http://astore.amazon.com/equipmentandtools-20

I hope you enjoy these recipes as much as my family and I do.

The next step is to attend a series of classes with me …

… to learn how to prepare even more delicious Raw Food!
It's time to invest in your health for prevention and to enjoy a richer lifestyle full of energy and fun!

Please check www.RawChefWendy.com/events for class dates and times.

THERE IS MORE AVAILABLE TO SUPPORT YOU

More Books

Online Programs

Private Chef Courses

Little Chef Summer Camp

Online Market

Monthly Newsletters

Magazine Articles

Television Appearances

Conferences

Retreats

& Much More!

Visit www.rawchefwendy.com and get involved.

www.ingramcontent.com/pod-product-compliance
Lightning Source LLC
Chambersburg PA
CBHW051247110526
44588CB00025B/2908